6 Hidden Behaviors That Destroy Families by Dr. Magdalena Battles is a practical tool for families of all sizes. Dr. Battles goes to great lengths to give practical instruction and specific examples that anyone can follow. The book is honest and presents real issues that families face, but it also gives deep encouragement for those willing to do the relational work. I *love* that one of the main themes I was left with was that all a family needs is one member to be the change!

—*Kendra Hunt*
Women's pastor
Author, *Encouragement Between Loads of Laundry*

Dr. Magdalena Battles hits it out of the park with *6 Hidden Behaviors That Destroy Families*. Her practical advice and scriptural references are spot-on. I couldn't agree more with her tips on how to be a good listener. My clients have seen their relationships transformed as they have followed Dr. Battles's advice on listening for understanding. I highly recommend this book!

—*Emily Eichstadt*
Speaker and certified life coach

In *6 Hidden Behaviors That Destroy Families*, Dr. Magdalena Battles uses her voice as a storyteller to walk alongside families as they navigate real-life struggles. Like the benefit of having regular fire drills, when we become familiar with the six major behaviors that destroy families and practice understanding them, we will become better equipped to deal with these issues if and when they flare up in our lives.

—*Shontell Brewer*
Author, *Missionary Mom*

Dr. Magdalena Battles illuminates systemic family issues that need to be proactively addressed in healthy and productive ways. I am grateful to have her wisdom, wit, engaging writing style, and relatable stories packaged in practical advice and counsel that can be a resource to families. *6 Hidden Behaviors That Destroy Families* is an easy read that gives clarity and definition to common family struggles, with a goal of repairing, reconciling, and fostering new, healthy dynamics. Dr. Battles has a heart of stewardship to help extended family members communicate and work through their issues in ways that foster meaningful connection.

—*Dr. Shannan Crawford*
Licensed psychologist, leadership consultant, conference speaker, and adjunct professor

Dr. Magdalena Battles's new book, *6 Hidden Behaviors That Destroy Families,* is an important work, offering practical solutions and biblically based teaching to foster a pleasant and supportive family environment. An expert in child development and a doctor of psychology, Dr. Battles knows her stuff. But more than that, she's a mom and a wife, a daughter-in-law, and a compassionate family member. Her personal story of struggle and the comfort she received from God as she learned valuable lessons give us hope that we can all achieve happy and healthy extended family relationships.

—*Paula Scott*
Author, *Farming Grace: A Memoir of Life, Love, and a Harvest of Faith*

6 Hidden Behaviors That Destroy Families is an easy but impactful *must*-read! On a personal note, I consider Dr. Magdalena Battles a friend and a woman of high character and calling. It was a privilege and joy to read her book because it was thought-provoking and challenging in the best possible way! As I read the wisdom she offers for navigating the challenges of relationships—with both family members and friends—I related to every chapter, and multiple stories in my own life came alive to me. One of my favorite features of this book is that it doesn't leave you a victim but instead equips you with practical tools to be the change agent in your life and in your family.

—*Stephanie Kelsey*
Groups pastor, Gateway Church, Southlake, TX

In *6 Hidden Behaviors That Destroy Families*, Dr. Magdalena Battles provides readers from all walks of life with a biblical worldview on how to develop effective relationships with their family members. She has a unique background as a professional psychologist who also has a spiritual understanding that we humans are created as three-part beings. We have a spirit, body, and soul, with the soul being the seat of our mind, will, and emotions. With this understanding, she is able to provide real solutions for family conflict that are built on the foundation of effective communication.

—*Paul Lodato*
General manager, Christian Television Network Southwest Florida
Florida Pastors Network

Dr. Magdalena Battles has laid a solid foundation and framework for healthy families. Her passion for unity in extended families is evident throughout this book, and her insight is valuable for any member of any family. If you have concerns about or issues with your family relationships, I highly recommend *6 Hidden Behaviors That Destroy Families*.

—*Kristin Lemus*
Founder, Brave Moms

I wish I'd had *6 Hidden Behaviors That Destroy Families* when I got married! And had kids! And became a supervisor! Both personally and professionally, I've had great success using the advice on mending and building relationships that Dr. Magdalena Battles gives in this book. Thank you, Dr. Battles, for helping us all by providing this resource in a format that is so easy to understand and apply.

—*Molly Lee*
Founder, Glory Gals

In her latest book, *6 Hidden Behaviors That Destroy* Families, Dr. Magdalena Battles uncovers the secrets behind a healthy family system. Through the real-life situations, biblical truth, and researched solutions she presents, you will learn how to have a family that functions in the way God intended it to—with peace and joy. I highly recommend this book for anyone in a family system, which is everyone!

—*Rachael Gilbert*
Marriage and family therapist, speaker, and author
Host, *Real Talk with Rachael* podcast

6 HIDDEN BEHAVIORS THAT DESTROY FAMILIES

STRATEGIES FOR HEALTHIER AND MORE LOVING RELATIONSHIPS

DR. MAGDALENA BATTLES

WHITAKER
HOUSE

Unless otherwise indicated, all Scripture quotations are taken from the *Holy Bible, New International Version*®, NIV®, © 1973, 1978, 1984, 2011 by Biblica, Inc.® Used by permission of Zondervan. All rights reserved worldwide. www.zondervan.com. The "NIV" and "New International Version" are trademarks registered in the United States Patent and Trademark Office by Biblica, Inc.® Scripture quotations marked (ESV) are taken from *The Holy Bible, English Standard Version*, © 2000, 2001, 1995 by Crossway Bibles, a division of Good News Publishers. Used by permission. All rights reserved. Scripture quotations marked (NASB) are taken from the updated *New American Standard Bible*®, NASB®, © 1960, 1962, 1963, 1968, 1971, 1972, 1973, 1975, 1977, 1995 by The Lockman Foundation. Used by permission. (www.Lockman.org). Scripture quotations marked (NKJV) are taken from the *New King James Version*, © 1979, 1980, 1982 by Thomas Nelson, Inc. Used by permission. All rights reserved. Scripture quotations marked (GNT) are taken from the *Good News Translation – Second Edition*, © 1992 by the American Bible Society. Used by permission. Scripture quotations marked (NCV) are taken from the *Holy Bible, New Century Version*®, © 2005 by Thomas Nelson, Inc. Used by permission. All rights reserved. Scripture quotations marked (CEB) are taken from the Common English Bible, copyright 2011. Used by permission. All rights reserved. Scripture quotations marked (NLT) are taken from the *Holy Bible, New Living Translation*, © 1996, 2004, 2007 by Tyndale House Foundation. Used by permission of Tyndale House Publishers, Inc., Carol Stream, Illinois 60188. All rights reserved.

The forms LORD and GOD (in small caps) in Bible quotations represent the Hebrew name for God *Yahweh* (Jehovah), while *Lord* and *God* normally represent the name *Adonai*, in accordance with the Bible version used.

The definition of *abuse* in chapter 2 is taken from Merriam-Webster.com, 2020. The definitions of *insult* in chapter 4 and *gossip* in chapter 6 are taken from Dictionary.com, 2020. The explanation of the Hebrew word translated *"choice morsels"* in chapter 6 comes from the Old Testament Hebrew Lexicon—King James Version or New American Standard, which is the Brown, Driver, Briggs, Genesius Lexicon (public domain), BibleStudyTools.com., and the electronic version of *Strong's Exhaustive Concordance of the Bible*, STRONG, (© 1980, 1986, and assigned to World Bible Publishers, Inc. Used by permission. All rights reserved.).

The abridged CaringBridge journal entry in chapter 1 and the excerpt from the Lifehack article "6 Big Mistakes That Destroy Family Relationships" in chapter 4 by Magdalena Battles have been lightly edited for this publication. Chapter 8, "When You Have Violated Someone's Trust," and chapter 9, "How to Recover from Broken Trust," were originally published by the author in a slightly different form as a single article on Lifehack entitled "How to Regain Broken Trust in a Relationship." The material has been revised and expanded to include biblical application and additional research. All material originally published on Lifehack used by permission. (www.lifehack.org).

6 HIDDEN BEHAVIORS THAT DESTROY FAMILIES:
Strategies for Healthier and More Loving Relationships

Dr. Magdalena Battles
DrErinMagdalena@hotmail.com
www.LivingJoyDaily.com

ISBN: 978-1-64123-443-6 • eBook ISBN: 978-1-64123-444-3
Printed in the United States of America
© 2020 by Magdalena Battles

Whitaker House • 1030 Hunt Valley Circle • New Kensington, PA 15068
www.whitakerhouse.com

Library of Congress Control Number: 2020935717

1 2 3 4 5 6 7 8 9 10 11 ᴸᴶ 27 26 25 24 23 22 21 20

CONTENTS

HIDDEN BEHAVIOR #5: A LACK OF INCLUSION

HIDDEN BEHAVIOR #6: A FAILURE TO ACCEPT DIFFERENCES

FOREWORD

I must have been only five or six years old when I asked, "Mamma, what happened to my grandparents?" My mother and I were driving home from my classmate's birthday party, hosted at her grandparents' home. The swim party had been a huge success, and I had watched as my friend received hugs, cuddles, and kisses from her doting grandparents throughout the two hours they served as hosts.

It had suddenly dawned on me that I had never seen my own grandparents, much less been showered with such obvious affection from them. My mom told me the truth about my grandparents in the best way she knew how. They were alive and well, living across town. They simply weren't a part of our lives. At the time, the explanation seemed odd, but I accepted it with childlike innocence.

Fast forward to 2020. I have more family members who are estranged from me than are in relationship with me, my husband, and our four beautiful sons. The seeds of bitterness, poor communication, and unforgiveness have sprouted and taken root for generations, and they have left a lifeless harvest of dead-end relationships that has fractured our family tree. This truth is one of the most painful realities of my life.

When I first met Dr. Magdalena Battles, I felt an overwhelming sense of well-being. Her nurturing spirit was straightforward and affirming. I immediately felt that this was someone who would have a positive influence on me. She was both wise and kind. It came as no surprise to learn she was a doctor of psychology and an expert in family relationships. Over the years, I have had the privilege to know her personally and call her a friend. When she handed me a copy of 6 *Hidden Behaviors That Destroy Families*, I felt like I was about to find hope and healing from my painful past. I was right! But reading this book didn't only accomplish these valuable results. It inspired me to disrupt the generational cycle of conflict and estrangement in my own little family. Magdalena gave me the much-needed insights and tools I had been desperate to find in order to break free from those chains so that my own children could one day experience the healthy and God-honoring design for family He had planned for them.

My grandparents passed away years ago. There is nothing I can do about the past, except to leave it there. However, this book has shown me how to proceed for the future. Magdalena doesn't give us a bunch of clichés or scenarios we can relate to and then leave us in our misery. She offers practical ideas to think about and implement for dealing with real-life problems like unforgiveness, gossip, and feeling left out of family events. Magdalena has made these big issues less fearsome and overwhelming by explaining life-giving principles from the Bible in a way that enables us to apply them to everyday situations with our extended family members. Already, I'm working through some of these practical ideas with my children, teaching them how to communicate better, respond with a kind tone of voice during conflicts, and put themselves in each other's shoes more often. I'm seeing the fruit of these conversations and it's generating in me an excitement about the future of our family that far outshines the pain of my past.

In my own books and ministry, I have noted the legacy of anger and frustration within many families around the world. 6 *Hidden Behaviors That Destroy Families* is the book we need to be reading *before* we escalate to the issues I write about—triggers that lead to angry reactions, which can do so much harm. But it's my belief that even for those of us who are squarely placed in the center of fractured families, following the advice in this book will bring healing and reconciliation.

Reading this book could be one of the most important things you do for yourself and your parents, spouse, siblings, in-laws, and children. God set us in our families with intention. He designed our children to be a blessing to us, our spouses to be a picture of unconditional love toward us, and our households to be a legacy of security and enrichment. As you read *6 Hidden Behaviors That Destroy Families*, you will receive the tools and encouragement you need to preserve and foster that godly design.

Read on with an open heart and an open mind. You're about to change your family legacy.

—*Amber Lia*
Best-selling coauthor, *Triggers, Marriage Triggers,*
and *Parenting Scripts*

PREFACE:
AN ARTICLE THAT WENT VIRAL

Families are complicated. There is no such thing as a perfect family…or an easy family. We all make mistakes that hurt or disappoint our extended family members, and we've all been hurt or disappointed by those we love. Yet within our human makeup is a deep and basic need for healthy family relationships. Family was designed to provide us with love, a feeling of belonging, a shared history, traditions, comfort, affection, quality time, feedback, learning, and a safety net. When our family fails to provide for these needs, we experience a sense of loss.

While every family has its problems—some minor, some major—what really matters is how we deal with these issues. Are we working to heal and resolve the conflicts, or are we allowing them to fester, divide, and explode, perhaps causing irreparable damage to our relationships?

We are either part of the problem or part of the solution. While doing nothing about a family issue may seem like the safest route, it often further contributes to the troubles. We have a choice to make: Do we want a family that is loving, supportive, and knows how to get along? Or do we want to continue along the path of hurt feelings, angry reactions, and severed communication? If we desire the first option, the good news is that we can help bring solutions and healing to our damaged families, regardless of the size of the problem.

TOP FAMILY CONFLICTS

I come from a large extended family, and I also have a doctorate in clinical and academic psychology. Several years ago, I wrote an article entitled "6 Big Mistakes That Destroy Family Relationships" for Lifehack, a top self-help website. The article went viral. I think people responded because they saw their own family problems clearly identified and explained to them for the first time. Even more than that, they could see both the issues and their solutions. Once we are able to pinpoint problems that are causing disagreement and strife in our immediate and extended families, we can work to solve them and make our relationships better and stronger.

6 Hidden Behaviors That Destroy Families is based on that Lifehack article. The behaviors are described as "hidden" because we often ignore, deny, or cover up our family issues. While volumes could be written about such problems, this book focuses on the top conflicts that cause relationships to become strained, disjointed, or broken. It also provides solutions for dealing with each damaging behavior. These solutions are drawn from my own life experiences, timeless principles from the Bible, solid research in psychology, and my professional observations of what works for families.

To help you better understand the issues and apply the corresponding solutions, I also share stories from my life and the lives of my family members, friends, and, at times, clients. Names have often been omitted or altered so individuals can remain anonymous. Other details not essential to the message of a particular story also may have been changed to conceal a person's identity.

I love my own extended family. However, just because I love them doesn't mean we haven't made mistakes and don't have problems. No, we certainly have our fair share. For example, some family members have gone through the pain of divorce and some have even gone to prison (some are still there). My extended family members come from varied religious backgrounds and income levels, and we have all made our own lifestyle choices. We are different people with distinct beliefs and values. However, we are also a family that knows how to get along—most of the time. (It would be impossible for any family to get along *all* of the time!) We overcome our differences and hurdle the hidden behaviors as they come. We are far from perfect, but we have found effective resolutions to our mistakes. I share them in this book because I want to help others who are going through similar situations.

You will find that there is some overlap in the advice that is given for the six hidden behaviors. While each behavior calls for its own approaches, there are certain principles of healing and restoration that are relevant to more than one behavior or are universally applicable. One example is the principle of forgiveness, which has the power to bring healing to both offender and offended.

A WORK IN PROGRESS

We must recognize that there is an ebb and flow to relationships. The family unit is a living organism, never remaining the same. Sometimes, it is healthy and working well, and other times, it is not as healthy or functional.

I admit that I don't do everything right with my own extended family, but I am trying. And I would never say that every relationship I have with my family members is great. That is an unrealistic expectation. It is important for us to recognize that we are *all* works in progress and need to be continually tending to our relationships. When we think everything is going great in our family life, that is usually when we become complacent and problems begin to surface. I know this pattern all too well. But my goal is to continually work through the mistakes I make with my family. I will continue to invest in my relationships because I know that God put each family member in my life for a significant reason. I hope you will make the same commitment.

Good relationships require time and effort. If we truly desire to have a loving extended family, then we need to be solution-focused and willing to take on our mutual problems. Let me assure you that you can be a means of bringing answers and healing to the damaged and broken relationships in your family. *6 Hidden Behaviors That Destroy Families* is designed to enable you to take the first steps. Yes, it is a process, but one that will result in happier lives and relationships, because love brings joy, acceptance, and goodwill. We can all be better people when we have family members who support and encourage us.

TAKE THOSE FIRST STEPS

Today is the day you can begin to bring love and healing to your family members. Even if you are the only one working on solving the problems, you will be making a difference. You may not think that your particular behavior matters because you are just one person in an extended family that may have a dozen or more members. However, you do matter. Whether your family is large or small, your actions influence others. Change often begins with one person. You can be the change that turns things around.

Please know that your loved ones are watching how you respond to challenges. Especially remember that the next generation is watching. They are learning from those around them about family dynamics and how to handle relationships within an extended family. Don't underestimate the generational difference you can make.

The way your family is today does not need to be the way it will be tomorrow, next year, or five years from now. If you want to have a family that knows how to treat its members appropriately and loves beyond measure, then continue reading. Remember, all it takes is one person to start a trend of love, compassion, and support that can change generations to come.

BLESSED IS THE INFLUENCE OF ONE TRUE, LOVING HUMAN SOUL ON ANOTHER.
—GEORGE ELIOT, ENGLISH NOVELIST

1

EVERY FAMILY HAS ISSUES

amily. We all have one—or had one at some point. Most of us have at least some living relatives. These may include a spouse, parents, siblings, grandparents, aunts, uncles, cousins, in-laws, and other extended family members. When you get together, do your family members generally show love, kindness, compassion, affection, and support toward one another? Or do they belittle and criticize each other, gossip, and hold grudges?

Family relationships, like all relationships, come with challenges. There is no such thing as a family without issues because every human being is fallible. This means each one of us has the potential to create a problem in our family! And unresolved problems in families can lead to hurt, strained relationships, and division.

YOU CAN BE A FAMILY HEALER

What many of us don't realize is that the issues our families deal with are often caused by hidden, destructive behaviors that the members have overlooked or never acknowledged. In this book, we will explore the top six hidden behaviors that destroy families. But we won't just look at the problems. We will discover proven strategies for healthier and more loving relationships. Together, we will walk the path to wholeness. Regardless of the issues we deal with, having a functioning family is within our grasp when we handle our mistakes in appropriate and positive ways.

You have the power to begin the process of healing and reconciliation. By discovering solutions to these six hidden behaviors, you can be the influence your family needs to improve and restore its relationships. Being a provider of answers to deep-rooted problems will make you a family healer.

THE SIX HIDDEN BEHAVIORS

Here are the six major hidden behaviors that can damage families to the core: (1) a failure to forgive or apologize, (2) criticism, (3) gossip, (4) deception, (5) a lack of inclusion, and (6) a failure to accept differences. Each section of *6 Hidden Behaviors That Destroy Families* contains tools and instructions to help you either avoid these behaviors or address them. As you read this book, you will find guidelines and principles you can apply directly to your particular circumstances. You will be empowered to more readily forgive and apologize, better handle constructive criticism, talk to family members directly rather than behind their backs, promote honesty and trust in interactions, include all members in gatherings and events, and accept each other's differences.

HAVING A FUNCTIONING FAMILY IS WITHIN OUR GRASP WHEN WE HANDLE OUR MISTAKES IN APPROPRIATE AND POSITIVE WAYS.

THE PAIN OF ESTRANGEMENT

Disagreements and division within the family can lead to various forms of separation between the members, such as giving or receiving the cold shoulder or experiencing a lack of intimacy due to unresolved hurts. The greater the intensity of the behaviors associated with the mistakes made, the deeper the damage. Often, this leads to one of the worst consequences of family conflict—estrangement.

I have experienced the pain of family separation, but I have also discovered effective ways estrangement can be mended when family members decide to love and be committed to one another. Let me share some of my personal story. My husband, Justin, and I had wanted to start a family as soon as we got married, and God blessed us with pregnancy right away. We had only been married for ten months when I gave birth to our first child, a son whom we named Barron Christian Battles.

Those first weeks at home as a family of three were bliss. However, when Barron was two weeks old, he stopped nursing. We took him to the local hospital, where I assumed we would see a lactation specialist. Instead, they transferred our son via ambulance to Marshfield (Wisconsin) Children's Hospital, which was an hour and a half away. That day, we had no idea that our lives would be changed forever.

We spent hours at the children's hospital seeing all sorts of specialists. Then, the head pediatric neurologist arrived to examine Barron. After the examination, we asked for her opinion on what was possibly wrong with him. Why had he stopped nursing? Why was he so weak? He looked healthy and normal, so there couldn't be anything too wrong with him. Right? She answered tentatively, stating that she thought he might have something called spinal muscular atrophy (SMA) type 1. She said they would run the SMA test, but it would take a few weeks to get the results. In the meantime, Barron would be tested for every other possible disease, disorder, or deficiency.

Late that evening, we checked into the local Ronald McDonald House.[1] I didn't go to sleep because I wanted to learn all I could about SMA. When I got on the Internet and googled this disease, I was horrified by what I read. It was among the worst possible news a parent could receive. On the very first website I came across, I discovered that SMA 1 is genetic and fatal for infants. Babies born with SMA 1 lived an average of five months.

I was so mentally drained from our long day that I could barely comprehend what I was reading. Wanting to find evidence that our son's condition did not match the signs and symptoms of this awful disease, I read many websites well into the night. However, I discovered that Barron exhibited all of the symptoms, including "frog legs,"[2] low muscle tone, a

---

1. Ronald McDonald House Charities is a nonprofit organization that provides support, temporary housing, and other resources for families while their children are undergoing medical treatment.
2. This term refers to "a frog-like position with the hips moved apart (abducted) and knees bent or flexed." "Werdnig-Hoffmann Disease," Rare Disease Database, National Organization for Rare Disorders (NORD), https://rarediseases.org/rare-diseases/werdnig-hoffmann-disease/.

decreasing ability to move his limbs, and bell-shaped lungs. We had been informed about this last symptom earlier in the day after the hospital took an X-ray. He fully fit the profile of an infant born with SMA. There was no cure. However, I still had hope. I also had some denial going on.

After ten grueling, emotionally draining days, we checked Barron out of the hospital. Not long afterward, our pediatrician called and asked us to come to her office to go over the test results. She confirmed that he had SMA and said there was currently no remedy. However, clinical trials were being conducted in other countries, such as China, in search of a cure. These trials gave us hope that our son might live at least a few more years. I held on to this hope and desperately sought out information about how to get him into the clinical studies.

Unfortunately, we never made it that far. When Barron was five weeks old, he went into cardiac arrest. He survived the episode but was put on life support at Children's Minnesota–Minneapolis Hospital. We still had hope that we would bring him home, but it didn't happen. His body succumbed to SMA, and he died in my arms when he was merely eight weeks old. On November 7, 2010, I wrote the following on our CaringBridge website page:

> Our little angel, Barron Christian Battles, went to heaven this evening at 11:15 p.m. He went peacefully in my arms to the Lord. It has been a touching experience to be present when our baby came into this world and also when he left. I am grateful for the time we had with him. Although it was short, we made the most of it.

> I don't even know how to explain what happened tonight, but I would like to share it anyway. Justin and I had requested to see Barron's pulmonologist to discuss our options. Barron had been heavily sedated for the past two days, so much so this afternoon that he appeared comatose. He had been in a lot of pain without the drugs, so they were necessary for his comfort. The doctor explained to us that with the medical equipment, we were just prolonging a painful situation—that Barron's body was telling us he was exhausted and would be in continual pain without the drugs. Knowing that our son had a terminal disorder and was

really struggling, Justin and I made the very difficult decision to remove respirator support at noon on Sunday. We both sobbed after making our decision, and the doctor left the room.

Just minutes after Barron passed this evening, I told Justin that people wouldn't believe what happened next. After the doctor left, Barron's heart rate instantly went from 180 to 60. He turned white and took very shallow breaths, and we knew it was his time. We called the pulmonologist back in. The doctor told us, "I guess he just needed your permission to go." We held Barron for the next hour, but he was gone within fifteen minutes. What was even more amazing (the Lord was really at work tonight), Justin's dad, Tim, had flown in from Atlanta, where he had been on a business trip, landing at 10:30 p.m. Barron had started to pass away at a little past 11:00 p.m., and we didn't know if Tim would get a chance to see him. But Tim came in and kissed Barron as he took his last few breaths. Barron also opened his eyes one last time, looked at Justin, myself, Tim, and Carol (Justin's mom), and then closed his eyes and went to heaven. We hadn't seen his eyes since early morning because of the sedation. It was a blessing from God that we were able to look into his eyes one last time as he said goodbye to us. We prayed as we held him, and we asked God to take our precious baby home.

...I never wanted my baby to die, but if I had to choose a way, it would be the way it happened tonight...no pain or suffering. He died peacefully in our arms and went home to meet Jesus.

Justin and I hadn't even been married a year, but our firstborn child had already been born and died. We were crushed emotionally. I didn't know how we were going to make it through this life-shattering tragedy. It was our faith in Christ that got us through, but our families also helped us.

I share this story of our tragedy because it was the hardest period of our married life and it was also the time when we needed our families the most. Both sides of our family were there for us. Each of Justin's siblings flew in from other states, as did his parents, several times over the eight weeks of Barron's life. My parents were a two-hour drive from the hospital in

Minneapolis and drove there almost every day for the three weeks Barron was there.

After our son passed away, our families not only supported us emotionally, but they also helped us by cooking meals, doing laundry, and assisting in making funeral arrangements. I don't know what we would have done without their seeing us through this tragic situation. They breathed life into us with their condolences and words of support. Their actions showed that they cared.

I will say this as gently as possible because I don't want to hurt current relationships. Our relationships with Justin's family had not always been smooth sailing. We had issues with them and they had issues with us. Again, every family has its problems, so I don't need to go into specifics. What I can say with all certainty and love is that they were there to love and support us in any way they could when Barron fell ill, when he passed away, and after he passed.

The way our families responded to Barron's passing was exactly what we needed in order to get through those devastating circumstances. Not only did we survive them, but we have now been married for over ten years and have three healthy children. God has blessed us greatly, and we know that someday we will be reunited with Barron in heaven and he will get to meet his siblings. We are very thankful that our families were by our side in the journey to overcome our loss.

LIFE-AND-DEATH SITUATIONS HELP US SEE THAT LIFE ON EARTH IS TEMPORARY AND WE NEED TO SUPPORT OUR LOVED ONES WHILE WE CAN.

I don't want to say that Barron's death happened for a particular reason, such as repairing the relationship with Justin's family. However, I do know that God can use horrible situations for His glory and our good. Barron got sick and died, but during that time, there was a restoration of extended family relationships. Healing occurred. Perhaps this happened because life-and-death situations often enable us to put things into perspective.

They help us see that life on earth is temporary and we need to support our loved ones while we can. We must let go of past hurts that have kept us from having healthy and loving relationships.

HOW WOULD YOU RESPOND?

I believe God can heal any situation. He has shown that He can use even something as tragic as death to bring people together again. It's up to us how we respond to the circumstances of our lives.

I have a friend who found out that her father was unfaithful to her mother by having an affair and fathering a child outside of marriage. My friend was only about eight years old at the time, and she didn't learn about the existence of her half-sister until they were both adults. Instead of reacting in anger and hatred, she chose to respond with grace. She connected with her half-sister, accepting and loving her as a new family member. Because of my friend's kind and caring response, she and her sibling have formed a friendship and bond.

My friend's father already knew that what he had done was wrong. He went to her and asked her to forgive him. She was willing to forgive, which means that she did not punish her father by withholding contact and severing the relationship. By forgiving, she has freed herself from additional negative emotions and their effects on her, her family, and even her health. But she has also asked her father to go with her to see a counselor so they can work through her intense feelings with professional support. In the meantime, she has gained a new sister because of her constructive response to her father's mistake. Her reaction is already affecting the next generation because both women have their own children, and the newfound cousins now have the opportunity to form lifelong friendships.

Another friend discovered that her late father's new wife had been his mistress for many years. Emails were found revealing that not only had the affair begun at least a decade earlier, but her father and stepmother had made great efforts to cover it up. Additionally, it had only been a year since my friend's mother had passed away. Her father had remarried right after her death. So, my friend lost both her parents within a short period of time.

Earlier, my friend had harbored suspicions that her father was having an affair and had attempted to discuss those suspicions with him, but he would never admit to any wrongdoing. Thus, she suffered two deep wounds after his passing. One wound was the fact of the affair and the other was the knowledge of his continued deception.

WITH A SECRET LIKE THAT, AT SOME POINT THE SECRET ITSELF BECOMES IRRELEVANT. THE FACT THAT YOU KEPT IT DOES NOT.

—SARA GRUEN, *WATER FOR ELEPHANTS*

My friend's opportunity to mend her relationship with her father died with him. Consequently, she is left with the harsh realization of how fallen a person he was. For his entire life, her father had appeared to many people to be a good Christian man, but he left behind a legacy of deceit and betrayal. If he had dropped his pride and asked his children for forgiveness, he might have left a legacy of honesty and redemption. Now, there will never be an apology, and his children's hearts are still wounded.

Can their hearts heal, even though they never received an apology from him? Yes, they can, with God's help. But the fracture left in the family may never be restored this side of heaven. After the truth came out, the relationship between my friend and her stepmother turned quite negative. To date, the stepmother has not taken any responsibility for her actions or offered an apology for her behavior. My friend is now focused on nurturing and guiding her own family to prevent a repetition of her father's transgression in the next generations. *"The Lord detests lying lips, but he delights in people who are trustworthy"* (Proverbs 12:22 NIV).

THERE ARE NO SECRETS THAT TIME DOES NOT REVEAL.

—JEAN RACINE, FRENCH PLAYWRIGHT

THE BREAKDOWN OF RELATIONSHIPS

Affairs, divorce, and family estrangement all result from hidden behaviors that are left uncorrected. Some people's estrangements involve the exclusion of only one or two family members, while others involve all family members. Some estrangements last for a short period of time, while others last for years or decades, creating substantial damage. However, not all instances of estrangement involve the devastating scenarios of deceit I have just described. They vary by individual and family and they occur over different types of conflict. The members' reactions to those situations and whether they attempt to mend their relationships can make or break a family. Although we cannot prevent all mistakes from occurring, we can respond to them in ways that bring healing and restoration.

Suppose two sisters haven't spoken to each other in years. As is typical, the sister who began the distancing blames the other sister, while the other sister insists the first sister is the guilty one. The sister who separated herself states that she couldn't endure her sibling's continual criticism every time they were together. She couldn't take another holiday filled with disapproval about how she wore her hair, raised her children, or kept her home. When she finally reached her limit for taking insults, her solution was to stop seeing this sister, even to the point of avoiding all family gatherings where her sibling was present.

The sisters' relationship broke down completely because one sibling couldn't stop criticizing and the other couldn't handle the criticism. But it isn't only their relationship that has suffered. The rest of the family members have also been negatively affected by the feud and the absence of the first sister at family gatherings. Additionally, because the sisters' families don't see each other, their children are growing up without knowing their cousins.

But what if the sisters had been able to get a handle on the issue before the first sibling reached her limit and the separation occurred? What if they had started making changes that worked toward restoration and drew their family back from the abyss of estrangement?

Health reporter Catherine Saint Louis wrote an article for the *New York Times* in which she examined a body of research on family relationships and dispelled some common myths about estrangement. One myth is that separation happens suddenly. According to the research, which focused on parents and adult children, estrangement occurs as a wearing down of relationships over the course of many years. Saint Louis writes, "It's usually a long, drawn-out process rather than a single blowout. A parent and child's relationship erodes over time, not overnight."[3] We saw a similar erosion of relationship in the illustration of the two sisters.

6 Hidden Behaviors That Destroy Families will not only help you learn to reestablish lapsed relationships but also to build strong family bonds as you effectively identify and deal with divisive issues. In this way, you can prevent the destructive effects of unhealthy interactions *before* they reach the point of estrangement. Hidden behaviors cause our families to slowly fall into disrepair. We need to be aware of this danger and become vigilant about maintaining our relationships.

FAMILY ESTRANGEMENT OCCURS AS A WEARING DOWN OF RELATIONSHIPS OVER THE COURSE OF MANY YEARS.

For My Thoughts are not your Thoughts, Nor are your ways My ways, says the Lord For as the heavens are higher than the earth so are My ways higher than your ways And My thoughts than your thoughts

THE GREATEST OF THESE IS LOVE

What is the right way to do anything, including building family relationships? My answer is always "God's way" because He is the ultimate expert in human suffering and relationship repair. As the Scriptures say, His ways are higher and better than ours. (See Isaiah 55:8–9.) That is why He can heal even the worst family conflicts that seem to us to be past repair. Nothing is beyond the power of God. If your family problems seem insurmountable, then begin to pray daily for your family members and the healing that He can bring.

God gave you a particular family for a reason. What you do with your relationships is important to Him and to you. And so, as we progress on this journey of healing and building family relationships, we will be looking

---

3. Catherine Saint Louis, "Debunking Myths About Estrangement," *New York Times*, December 20, 2017, https://www.nytimes.com/2017/12/20/well/family/debunking-myths-about-estrangement.html.

at principles from God's Word that will help us respond to family conflict in constructive ways. The most important principle, which is foundational for all the others, was stated by Jesus when He was asked to name the greatest commandment in the Law:

> *You shall love the Lord your God with all your heart and with all your soul and with all your mind. This is the great and first commandment. And a second is like it: You shall love your neighbor as yourself. On these two commandments depend all the Law and the Prophets.*
> (Matthew 22:37–40 ESV)

Life is all about loving others. We were designed by God to have loving relationships, and this is also our calling. The greatest commandments are to love God and other people. This obviously includes our family members. They are our primary "neighbors." Loving others should begin with them because God has placed our family members in our lives and these are the people with whom we usually form our first and closest connections. If we marry and have children, we gain additional family members to whom we have special lifelong commitments.

Paul the apostle wrote, *"And now these three remain: faith, hope and love. But the greatest of these is love"* (1 Corinthians 13:13). The greatest, most life-giving asset we can provide another person is love. However, we have seen how love can be damaged when negative behaviors become a pattern and are left unresolved. Over time, these behaviors can create so much damage that relationship growth comes to a stop. Contact between individuals ceases to exist. Families become broken. This is not God's desire for His children.

First Timothy 5:8 shows the priority God places on caring for our families:

> *Anyone who does not provide for their relatives, and especially for their own household, has denied the faith and is worse than an unbeliever.*
> (1 Timothy 5:8)

Providing for your household is not limited to supplying food, clothing, and shelter. It also includes providing love and kindness. Love—practical, deep, and enduring—is the answer to your family problems. You can start loving your family today, as God has called us all to do. Often, this requires resilience and perseverance. Yet when you take God's Word to heart and implement it in your life, you will see encouraging results.

TAKE AN ACTIVE ROLE

We can't control the behavior of others, but we can control our own behavior and responses. Family healing is indeed possible, even in complicated scenarios of estrangement, because God is still in the business of doing miracles. Don't give up hope! Take an active role in preventing and healing the discord, dysfunction, and disenfranchisement that can result from the six hidden behaviors that destroy families. Once again, those behaviors are a failure to forgive or apologize, criticism, gossip, deception, a lack of inclusion, and a failure to accept differences.

You *can* learn successful strategies for avoiding and correcting negative behaviors. You relationships *can* become healthier, more loving, and supportive. Whatever mistakes have already happened, make a decision to promote forgiveness and reconciliation. Recognizing your mistakes is the first step toward healing. As soon as you become aware of and identify the cause of the dysfunction, healing can begin. Partner with God today and take action to become a family healer.

CHRISTIAN FAITH IS...BASICALLY ABOUT LOVE AND BEING LOVED AND RECONCILIATION. THESE THINGS ARE SO IMPORTANT, THEY'RE FOUNDATIONAL AND THEY CAN TRANSFORM INDIVIDUALS, FAMILIES.

—PHILIP YANCEY, INTERVIEW WITH THE *CHRISTIAN POST*

ARE YOU DEALING WITH ESTRANGEMENT?

If you are dealing with deep or long-standing family estrange-ment, the information in this book will be very beneficial, but professional assistance is also recommended. Support groups, therapy, or counseling can help. You may find that reconciliation is possible over time or you may not. You won't know until you try. You may be unwilling to reconcile because of abuse, neglect, abandonment, or other reasons. This is understandable. However, it still doesn't erase the hurt that you will experience from family estrangement, even if you are the person who justifiably doesn't want the reconciliation.

Dr. Lucy Blake of the University of Cambridge conducted research on family estrangements in collaboration with Professor Susan Golombok, director of the Centre for Family Research at Cambridge and Becca Bland of the Stand Alone organization, a charity that focuses on supporting adults who are experienc-ing family estrangement. Their study included more than eight hundred participants, all of whom were members of the Stand Alone community and had self-identified as being estranged from their entire family or a significant family member. More than three-quarters of the participants had received counseling or ther-apy, and 54 percent of that number found the support very helpful, while another 34 percent found it somewhat helpful. About one-fifth of participants had sought help from a Stand Alone support group, and 93 percent of them found the group helpful.[4]

It is important for you to find a counselor, therapist, or sup-port group that is empathetic to your situation. Not all counselors and therapists are equal. If one doesn't help you as you would like, try another. Don't give up on your pursuit of emotional healing. Isolating yourself and pretending you don't have a problem are among the worst things you can do to yourself. You will likely suffer sadness, depression, physical health issues, and other problems if

---

4. "Hidden Voices: Family Estrangement in Adulthood," University of Cambridge Centre for Family Research and Stand Alone, https://www.standalone.org.uk/wp-content/uploads/2015/12/HiddenVoices.FinalReport.pdf.

you cut yourself off from other people. Be sure to maintain the relationships you have developed outside of your family, as they can be helpful when going though family estrangement.[5] Reach out to a friend, colleague, or clergyperson. Again, not everyone is as helpful as we would like them to be or is able to see things from our perspective, so find people in your life who can be true supports to you.

---

5. "Family Estrangement: Advice and Information for Parents," Stand Alone and Dr. Joshua Coleman, 2015, https://www.standalone.org.uk/guides/parents/.

CHAPTER RECAP

This book covers the top six hidden behaviors that are sources of destruction to families: a failure to forgive or apologize, criticism, gossip, deception, a lack of inclusion, and a failure to accept differences. In Matthew 22:37–40, Jesus tells us that the greatest commandments are to love God and to love others. A family is the opposite of loving when its members engage in negative behavior that damages or destroys their relationships. One of the worst consequences of family conflict is estrangement.

There are effective strategies that can help bring about healing and restoration in families. The process can begin with one family member making the effort to be the agent of change and become a family healer. That person can be you.

QUESTIONS FOR REFLECTION

1. What negative behaviors have your family members engaged in that have damaged relationships? Which have been the most destructive? Were they among the six major behaviors discussed in this book?

2. Have you ever behaved in a way that resulted in damage to a family relationship? What was this behavior? Did you work to resolve the problem? If so, what was the outcome?

3. Are you willing to be a solution-oriented family member who can help restore and repair your family relationships? Will you commit to being an agent of change for your family?

HIDDEN BEHAVIOR #1:

A FAILURE TO FORGIVE OR APOLOGIZE

2

THE BENEFITS OF FORGIVENESS

Are you part of a family in which no one ever apologizes? Or do you have certain family members who refuse to apologize, even when they are egregiously wrong? I am not going to speak negatively of anyone, but I will say that I can relate to having loved ones who don't apologize after mistreating others. Instead, they simply go on with life, acting friendly and cordial, as if the situation never happened. As a result, the offenses they committed are never addressed.

This behavior completely baffled me the first time I experienced it, especially because I tend to be vocal. Ignoring the elephant in the room is not how I operate. Since then, I have come to understand this type of behavior. This makes it easier for me to forgive and move forward, even if words of apology are never expressed. The other person's extension of an olive branch and kindness toward me is their way of communicating an apology and showing a desire to restore the relationship.

I appreciate the fact that they want to mend the relationship and can even do so without speaking specific words about their offense. However, their response is not ideal. Words carry weight. In situations in which forgiveness is needed, a combination of sincere words and authentic actions works best. In chapter 3, we will discover how to apologize in the right way after we have offended or wronged someone. This chapter is devoted to the benefits of forgiveness on our part when we are the one who has been wronged.

FORGIVENESS IS IN OUR BEST INTEREST

When there is a lack of forgiveness, a wall goes up between the parties involved. Healthy relationships include both apologies and forgiveness. God calls us to forgive in all circumstances. The following passage from the book of Matthew speaks clearly on the subject of forgiveness:

> *For if you forgive other people when they sin against you, your heavenly Father will also forgive you. But if you do not forgive others their sins, your Father will not forgive your sins.*   (Matthew 6:14–15)

What if the person never apologizes for their behavior? Then, we are to forgive them in our heart, even if we never have an opportunity to express our forgiveness toward them. God wants us to forgive others for our own sake as well as theirs. When we harbor ill will over a wrong someone committed against us, it can cause a bitterness that grows and festers. Until we release that bitterness by truly forgiving the other person, we will suffer emotionally and even mentally. God doesn't want us to hurt and suffer. He wants us to release our burden to Him so He can heal our heart.

TO FORGIVE IS TO SET A PRISONER FREE AND DISCOVER THAT THE PRISONER WAS YOU.
—LEWIS B. SMEDES, AUTHOR, THEOLOGIAN, AND ETHICIST

Harboring ill feelings against someone can also have a harmful effect on our body. Negative thoughts and emotions bring about negative reactions within us. When we continually think about a wrong someone committed against us, thus permitting anger and resentment to build, our anxiety and stress levels go up. Those feelings obviously do not foster good health.

For example, if you are angry because you found out your sister-in-law has been saying bad things about you to your neighbor, and you have allowed that negative emotion to fester for months, you are compounding the detrimental effects of that emotion. You are also keeping yourself in a place of negativity. Learn to forgive and let it go. Talk to your sister-in-law if you feel comfortable doing so. If not, then you need to move forward for the sake of your own emotional and physical wellness.

> Studies have found that the act of forgiveness can reap huge rewards for your health, lowering the risk of heart attack; improving cholesterol levels and sleep; and reducing pain, blood pressure, and levels of anxiety, depression and stress. And research points to an increase in the forgiveness-health connection as you age....
>
> One study found that people whose forgiveness came in part from understanding that no one is perfect were able to resume a normal relationship with the other person, even if that person never apologized.[6]

This last result is huge! Research shows we need to recognize that nobody is perfect. Mistakes are part of being human. The Bible repeatedly tells us this fact. It says we all miss the mark; we are all sinners. How can we expect forgiveness from God and other people if we ourselves are unwilling to forgive? It is a double standard. Science and Scripture both point us toward what we should do when we are wronged in relationships. Forgiveness is in our best interests.

HOW CAN WE EXPECT FORGIVENESS FROM GOD AND OTHER PEOPLE IF WE OURSELVES ARE UNWILLING TO FORGIVE?

Professor Robert D. Enright of the University of Wisconsin developed a scientifically proven forgiveness program. His research revealed that when genuine forgiveness occurs, there is emotional healing and pain is released. Enright found that forgiveness is beneficial to both parties involved. It is not a one-sided experience. Genuine forgiveness heals the heart of the one

---

6. "Forgiveness: Your Health Depends on It," Johns Hopkins Medicine, https://www. hopkinsmedicine.org/health/wellness-and-prevention/forgiveness-your-health-depends-on-it.

who has hurt another and it also dissolves the pain in the person who has been hurt. Forgiveness allows both parties to regain their lives. It is essential to making a relationship whole again.[7]

FORGIVENESS DOESN'T MEAN CONDONING THE WRONG

When we forgive someone, it is not the same as condoning their actions. For example, suppose your brother borrowed a thousand dollars from you and promised to pay you back when he received his next paycheck. It has now been a full year and he still has not repaid you. At the time, you needed that money for your own bills, and he put you in a tough situation for a couple of months. Forgiving your brother doesn't mean you disregard the fact that he hasn't repaid the loan. It means you don't hold any anger, resentment, or bitterness against him because he borrowed money and failed to reimburse you. It means you let go of those feelings of ill will and take the situation as a life lesson.

The lesson is that you won't put yourself in a position to lend your brother money again because he can't be counted on to pay you back. Just because you forgive doesn't mean you can't act wisely in subsequent financial matters. You survived the situation and your bills eventually got paid. Your brother is still family and you need to love him. Holding on to bitterness and anger will certainly kill love. You might talk to him about what happened and express your forgiveness while letting him know you won't be able to lend him money again. You can allow him a chance to explain and make things right, but you should make a commitment to forgive either way.

FORGIVENESS IS A PROCESS

We need to recognize that, in most situations, forgiving someone in our heart takes time. It is not instant. The amount of time it takes to fully forgive usually correlates with the severity of the offense. If someone killed your child, your ability to forgive them fully in your heart will obviously

---

7. Robert D. Enright, *Forgiveness Is a Choice: A Step-by-Step Process for Resolving Anger and Restoring Hope* (Washington, DC: APA LifeTools, American Psychological Association), 2001.

take a great deal of time and effort, as compared to forgiving a friend for a minor fault, such as missing a lunch date with you.

We can make the decision to forgive in our heart, but it is human nature to have a mixture of emotions arise within us when we are reminded of the offense, even after we have consciously chosen to release the other person. For example, suppose your husband cheated on you. You have forgiven him and gone to counseling, both by yourself and together. As a result, there has been much healing in your marriage and a strengthening of your bond. However, when you go out for date nights, it sometimes seems as if he is eyeing other women, even if it is just a flicker of a look. In those moments, all of your anger and bitterness about his past affair comes boiling to the surface. These are the times when you especially need to pray and ask God to help you overcome the feelings that are eating at you. They aren't affecting your spouse. You are only hurting yourself when you continually allow yourself to dwell on those emotions.

You can make a conscious choice not to wallow in your negative feelings any longer. Wallowing is when you allow yourself to throw your own pity party, but that only fuels the emotions. Don't throw fuel on your feelings. It is okay to recognize that your emotions are natural. However, also remind yourself that you made the decision to put the issue behind you. Moving forward, your relationship will only be healthy if you choose not to focus on your hurt feelings. If they arise often, a therapist, counselor, or psychologist can greatly assist in your healing by helping you process your feelings so that you aren't constantly dealing with the same emotions from past hurts.

FORGIVENESS IS NOT AN OCCASIONAL ACT; IT IS A PERMANENT ATTITUDE.
MARTIN LUTHER KING JR.

WHAT ABOUT REPEAT OFFENDERS?

What if someone repeatedly commits the same offense against you? That's a tough situation. It makes forgiveness much more difficult.

However, it is possible. God calls us to forgive others even when they continually sin against us. This is what Jesus taught His disciple Peter about forgiving repeat offenders:

> *Then Peter came to Jesus and asked, "Lord, how many times shall I forgive my brother or sister who sins against me? Up to seven times?" Jesus answered, "I tell you, not seven times, but seventy-seven times."*
> (Matthew 18:21–22)

Forgiving repeat offenders is easier said than done. But when God tells us to do something, we need to do it for the sake of our relationship with Him and obedience to His Word. Remember, forgiveness is for our benefit as well. It helps to heal our own hearts.

HOW TO PROTECT YOURSELF FROM FUTURE OFFENSES

Even so, you need to take steps to protect yourself from being mistreated. You don't have to expose yourself to someone who wrongs you on a regular basis. God didn't say we must continue to allow someone to sin against us, but only that we are to forgive them when they do sin against us. It is up to us to set boundaries so the person doesn't have the opportunity to constantly commit offenses against us.

For example, suppose your mother-in-law insults you whenever you are around her. You forgive her in your heart, but the insults still hurt. You want the comments to stop so you can enjoy your time together more. Making her aware of your feelings is the first and foremost step. You can go to her directly and explain how her words hurt you and affect your relationship with her. Tell her how you feel, but do not give an ultimatum. Simply ask her to stop insulting you. You might be shocked at how many people are oblivious to their own behavior and the effect it has on the people around them.

We don't always understand people's motivations for their actions. Your mother-in-law may be putting you down because her own daughter struggles in her roles as a wife and mom, while you are thriving in those roles, so she is jealous. In order to make herself feel better about her daughter, she insults you about anything she can think of when you are around.

Perhaps you go on a weekend trip with your close friends from college, and your husband takes care of the children while you are away. After you return, your mother-in-law tells you that you abandoned your young children at home. She may be thinking, "I'm glad my own daughter doesn't do those girls' trips and instead takes care of her kids. Even if she isn't the best mom, at least she is there for them." Not knowing her thoughts, your interpretation of her negative comment is that she generally disapproves of you as a wife and mother.

Having a courteous but honest conversation with your mother-in-law to let her know you don't appreciate her put-downs could open a dialogue between the two of you about her behavior and its effect on you. If people aren't aware of a problem, how can we expect them to change?

Setting the stage for the conversation is paramount. You might approach her by saying you want to talk to her because she is family, you love her, and you want to have a great relationship long-term, so you desire to improve your rapport with her. If she thinks you are criticizing or attacking her, it is unlikely she will open up. Instead, she will become defensive. Help her to open up emotionally by making yourself vulnerable too. Admit that you are hurt and you care what she thinks because she is an important person in your life. You will not be able to control her reaction, but you can do your best to set the conversation up for success.

If your mother-in-law doesn't see any problem with the way she talks to you and it becomes clear she doesn't want to change, then you have a decision to make. You can either continue to allow yourself to be insulted or you can create boundaries so you don't leave yourself open to degrading comments. If boundaries have to be set, then you will need to let her know about them. Of course, these decisions should be made with your husband. At the same time, you will need to continually extend forgiveness toward your mother-in-law in your heart.

YOU DON'T HAVE TO EXPOSE YOURSELF TO SOMEONE WHO WRONGS YOU ON A REGULAR BASIS.

One example of a boundary is to tell her that if she insults you while you are visiting her home or the home of another relative, then you and your family will have to leave. In the beginning, she might feel like she is walking on eggshells around you. However, that may need to happen for her to change her behavior. It will help her become aware of her tendency to insult you. If she chooses to continue the insults, then more boundaries might need to be put in place. For example, you might limit your exposure to her and her comments to only a couple of times a year. Your husband and children can visit your in-laws more often, but you will be spared the constant put-downs.

As we will discuss more fully in chapter 4, insults are different from criticism. Insults are abusive, whereas constructive criticism is often given because the person loves you and wants to help you. One definition of the verb *abuse* is "to use or treat so as to injure or damage." If someone is continually insulting you and it is damaging to your soul and overall well-being, they are abusing you. I could list many other scenarios of mistreatment.

Don't allow yourself to be subject to mistreatment. Stay away from people who abuse you and are unwilling to change. However, as in the example of the mother-in-law's verbal abuse, do give the person an opportunity to change. They might not know that change is needed or be motivated to change unless you address the problem with them. If they love you and want a positive relationship, then they will make an effort to behave differently. (In later chapters, we will explore in more detail the process of going to someone when they have wronged us, based on Jesus's instructions in Matthew 18.)

HOLDING A GRUDGE DOESN'T MAKE YOU STRONG;
IT MAKES YOU BITTER.
FORGIVING DOESN'T MAKE YOU WEAK;
IT SETS YOU FREE.
—DAVE WILLIS, *THE SEVEN LAWS OF LOVE*

Suppose your mother-in-law initially balked at your feelings, thinking there was nothing wrong with her behavior. However, several days later, she comes to you and apologizes. First, she asks for your forgiveness. Then, she makes a commitment to cease the behavior, saying she will no longer make negative comments, including criticizing your parenting style. She assures you that if you ever want her advice on anything, you can ask her, but she won't provide any that is not requested. The apology is especially meaningful in this situation because of her commitment not to criticize in the future. Her actions show that she cares about you and is willing to make the effort to improve the relationship.

It is remarkable the way giving some people time to reflect can help them come to the right conclusions. When most people hear negative statements about their behavior, they react with defensiveness. However, this is when you need to allow them time to think and consider the situation outside of your conversation.

Unfortunately, not everyone wants positive relationships. Some people are stuck in patterns of maltreatment. It might be all they know. Or, for whatever reason, they might be unwilling to let go of the burden of the abusive behavior they carry. Let me repeat: don't allow yourself to continue to be mistreated if the other person is unwilling to change. However, you need to do your part by ensuring that they know the problem exists and extending forgiveness.

THE BEST WAY TO CHANGE PEOPLE IS
NOT BY RIDICULE BUT BY SHOWING THEM A
NEW WAY OF THINKING, AND GIVING THEM AN
OPPORTUNITY FOR CHANGE.
—AUTHOR UNKNOWN

CHAPTER RECAP

When there is a lack of forgiveness in a relationship, a wall goes up between the two parties. Healthy relationships include both apologies and forgiveness. God calls us to forgive each other:

> *For if you forgive other people when they sin against you, your heavenly Father will also forgive you. But if you do not forgive others their sins, your Father will not forgive your sins.*   (Matthew 6:14–15)

When we don't forgive others, not only does it damage our relationships, but it also creates emotional, mental, and physical problems for us. We need to forgive for the sake of our relationships and our overall well-being. This is the case even if the other person never acknowledges their wrongdoing or apologizes.

QUESTIONS FOR REFLECTION

1. Is there someone in your family who wronged you but never apologized? How is your relationship with that person? If the relationship is strained, what might you do to bring healing and reconciliation between you?

2. How do you handle forgiveness when a person doesn't apologize? How might you handle it better?

3. In what ways should you respond to someone who continually wrongs you?

3

HOW TO APOLOGIZE IN THE RIGHT WAY

Offering an apology after you have wronged another person does not come easy to everyone. Some people really struggle with the art of apologizing. If that is true of you, this chapter will help you learn how to apologize in the right way and with the best chance of restoring your relationship. Since apologizing can be so difficult, we first must understand why it is necessary.

WHY SHOULD WE APOLOGIZE?

Apologizing is your way of telling someone they are important in your life and you want to heal the relationship by acknowledging your wrongdoing. When you don't offer an apology and show no remorse for your actions, it conveys to the other person that they don't mean much to you.

Apologizing is also your verbal commitment to righting your wrong. An apology starts with admitting you did something that hurt the other person, and it is complete when you formally ask for forgiveness and let them know you will change and not hurt them in that way again.

GUIDELINES FOR APOLOGIZING

EXPRESS GENUINE REMORSE

If you are truly sincere in your apology, that message will come through. If you are not, that message will be obvious as well. Most people can tell whether others are being genuine. This is a general instinct and judgment call we all make when someone is communicating with us. Much of it has to do with nonverbal cues from the other person. You may not even be able to explain exactly what caused you to disbelieve the sincerity of another person and what they were saying to you. You just know that something was not quite right and your trust flags went up. The person might have said all the right words, but their behavior somehow gave away their true emotions and thoughts. They might even have been trying to convince themselves of their sincerity as they apologized, but you could tell they weren't being completely honest.

I believe each person has a "tell" that indicates when they are not being genuine. I have an acquaintance who gives half-truths. I think she does this because she is afraid others will judge her choices. She will talk very hurriedly, act dismissive of any questions, and avoid eye contact. It is as if she is in a rush to get the conversation over with because she is uncomfortable with these half-truths. I know someone else who acts hostile when he is being dishonest. His way of dealing with his lack of truthfulness is to become defensive and then try to turn the tables on the other person to point out their faults.

**NEVER FORGET THE NINE MOST IMPORTANT
WORDS OF ANY FAMILY—
I LOVE YOU.
YOU ARE BEAUTIFUL.
PLEASE FORGIVE ME.**
—JACKSON BROWN, *LIFE'S LITTLE INSTRUCTION BOOK*

You will find that if you pay attention to the behavior of your family members, you can learn their "tells." Is there someone in your family with whom you have trust issues? Think back to a conversation or situation when you recall they were not being entirely truthful. What kind of verbal or nonverbal behaviors did they exhibit during the exact time they were being dishonest?

Your family members can likewise learn to recognize your "tells." Therefore, when you offer an apology, remember that your loved ones are probably going to pick up on any disingenuousness. Family members can usually spot our dishonesty cues more easily than other people can because they know us best. If your promises to change are hollow, they will know it. In contrast, if your promises are sincere, they will sense it. So, be honest and genuine. That is the only way you can build good relationships with your family members and others.

CHECK YOUR TONE OF VOICE AND BODY LANGUAGE

Sincerity comes across not only in the words we use but also in the tone of voice and body language we employ. Blake Eastman is a specialist in nonverbal communication, and he says that a majority of our communication is nonverbal:

> Based on my own research, I would state that the amount of communication that is nonverbal varies between 60 and 90% on a daily basis. This number depends on both the situation and the individual.[8]

This means that what you *aren't* saying can communicate even more than your words. For example, when you apologize, do you look at the floor, or even worse, your phone? You need to look the wronged individual in the eyes to communicate your sincerity. If you can't meet with them in person because you live too far away, then the next best thing is a video chat or phone call.

Texting an apology does not convey sincerity. I have been guilty of that in the past. It is so easy to text, and texting has become a primary mode of communication for many people. However, in a situation where you are asking for forgiveness, what texting can communicate to the other person is that they aren't worth the time and energy of a phone call to apologize.

The tone of a message sent via text or email can also easily be misinterpreted. Read the following sentence out loud in a harsh or indifferent tone: "I'm sorry I missed our lunch date. I had an appointment and so much to

---

8. Blake Eastman, "How Much of Communication Is Really Nonverbal?" The Nonverbal Group, http://www.nonverbalgroup.com/2011/08/how-much-of-communication-is-really-nonverbal.

do today that I forgot." Now, read the sentence out loud again, using a sincere and apologetic tone of voice, expressing that you regret having missed lunch with your favorite person in the whole world.

Tone can make such a difference! That is why face-to-face communication is the best way to make a sincere apology.

WHAT YOU *AREN'T* SAYING CAN COMMUNICATE EVEN MORE THAN YOUR WORDS.

FOCUS ON THE HURT YOU CAUSED, NOT THE OTHER PERSON'S FAULTS

Be honest when you apologize, but do so with love and kindness. Honesty does not mean being blunt in expressing what you did or reminding the other person of their own failings. Suppose you told your brother you would be attending your nephew's piano recital but then forgot about it. When you apologize, omit bringing up the fact that he missed your daughter's flute recital earlier in the year, saying, "Yeah, sorry I missed the piano recital, but you missed Anna's performance last spring." That approach would not be helpful. Don't undercut your apology or make it less sincere by talking about ways the other person has similarly hurt you.

Here's another illustration. Imagine you borrowed your sister's dress for an event and stained it, but instead of having it cleaned, you gave it back in that spoiled condition. You should apologize and make things right. (Later in this chapter, we will discuss making things right in more depth.)

This is how *not* to make the apology: "I'm sorry I stained your dress and returned it that way, but you borrowed my earrings a few months back and I never saw them again, so we can call it even." That is not the right mindset. You may feel justified in this approach. However, will such a declaration heal your relationship, or will it simply make you feel on an equal level or even superior to your sister for a fleeting moment? We say things like this to try to create an even playing field, wanting the other person to know they aren't so innocent either. They have offended us in the past and we'd like to remind them of that fact. We probably take this approach more often than we realize.

Yet the other person is already feeling hurt by us for the current situation. Then we bring up offenses *they* have committed against us. Their reaction is likely to be defensive. Once their self-protective walls go up, the apology process is greatly hindered. Arguing, blaming, and bringing up past transgressions have no place in an apology. They will only detract from it and make you seem insincere. So, resist the urge to bring up previous wrongs the other person has done to you. Remember that two wrongs don't make a right. God can see through to your heart, and He will note your actions.

DON'T UNDERCUT YOUR APOLOGY OR MAKE IT LESS SINCERE BY TALKING ABOUT WAYS THE OTHER PERSON HAS SIMILARLY HURT YOU.

Our enemy, Satan, would like nothing more than for our relationships with our loved ones to be destroyed. Jesus said,

The thief enters only to steal, kill, and destroy. I came so that they could have life—indeed, so that they could live life to the fullest.
(John 10:10 CEB)

Satan wants to make you think you are justified in bringing up the other person's wrongdoing, but that's because he wants to attack your relationships. Don't let him have any victory in your life.

Are your relationships more important to you than your need to feel justified or superior to someone else? They should be because, at the end of the day, when you are the one taking the high road and doing what is right and good, your relationships will flourish.

Returning to the example of borrowing your sister's dress and staining it, instead of tossing blame at your sibling, here is a more appropriate response that can bring restoration and harmony once again: "I'm sorry I stained your dress and returned it that way. It was wrong of me. I want to make things right. I will pay for the dry-cleaning bill, so please let me take it to the cleaners or let me know how much I owe you." When you make things right, it will create a better relationship in the long run.

In such a situation, you can also give the other person the benefit of the doubt. Rather than assuming your sister lost the earrings or doesn't care about returning them, ask her about them. However, do so later, in a separate conversation apart from the stained-dress discussion. The best time to inquire is not when things are already heated or you are talking about another wrong. Otherwise, the conversation will likely deteriorate and become a quarrel about all the wrongs you have ever committed against each other and who has the most ammunition. Nobody wins in that situation. Yes, you might feel justified for a few minutes, but then you would be left with additional hurt feelings and a deeper chasm between the two of you. In that later conversation, when you inquire if she happens to still have the earrings she borrowed from you, you may learn that she had completely forgotten about them and is ready to give them back to you. You won't know unless you ask.

That is why, to help you focus on the hurt you have caused rather than the other person's faults, you should check to see if you are harboring anger or resentment against them for something in the past. If so, then, before apologizing, release it to God so you can forgive this person in your heart. Remember that God can help you forgive and move forward whether the other person has apologized or not, but you must first recognize you are holding on to anger or resentment.

If past hurts seem to come to your mind whenever you have arguments or heated discussions with an individual, this shows you are still harboring resentment or bitterness against them. Refuse to bring up those issues while having a disagreement about something else. As we have seen, it clearly will not help to heal or resolve anything.

Keep in mind that at another time, you can bring up issues of concern to you if they are creating a wall between you and your family member. If the other person loves you, they will want that wall to come down too. They may not even know that the issue from the past is still bothering you. When you have that separate conversation, give them the opportunity to apologize.

In the meantime, focus on the hurt that *you* caused. It's like the old saying from school days: "Keep your eyes on your own paper." Look only at what you have done to offend the other person. Put yourself in their shoes and think hard about how you would feel if that hurt were inflicted on you. Convey your sincerest apology by expressing remorse for your actions and the harm you have caused.

ACKNOWLEDGE YOUR WRONG

The other person's feelings count, so don't be dismissive toward them. If someone you love says you hurt them for one reason or another, then take that information to heart. Everyone is entitled to their own feelings. You can't say to someone, "You don't have the right to feel hurt." Often, they do. You do, too, when you have been wronged. But remember, the focus at the time of an apology should be on the hurt you have caused, so that you can make things right in the relationship on your end.

Therefore, when you ask for forgiveness, you should fully admit you have wronged the other person as you acknowledge the feelings of hurt this has caused them. This discussion is about them, their feelings, and the restoration of your relationship. For instance, if you are apologizing for neglecting to invite a family member to a recent family gathering, you need to acknowledge how your actions injured them. Don't try to justify your behavior.

This is an example of what *not* to say: "I'm sorry we didn't include you at our family dinner, but we just assumed you wouldn't want to come because you are always so busy and can't make most gatherings." Such a response makes it seem like you are trying to excuse your conduct and even place the blame on the other person. That won't work to mend hurt feelings. It will probably make the individual feel like you really didn't want to invite them and now you don't want to own up to it. Even if they have declined every other dinner invitation, don't bring up that fact. It is not the time or place and it will truly make you look less apologetic. If your desire is a good family relationship, then just say you are sorry without any excuses or blame. Recognize the other person's feelings in the way you word your apology.

Here is a suggestion for a better way to apologize in such a situation: "I am sorry I didn't invite you to the family dinner. It was a terrible mistake. I know you are hurt that you weren't included and I am sorry I caused you that hurt. I promise it won't happen again. You are a part of this family and will be invited to all family dinners in the future." Acknowledging their feelings helps them see that you truly understand their perspective. They want to know that you comprehend their point of view and the hurt they are experiencing. The way they will know you understand how they feel is when you specifically state those feelings to them.

RECOGNIZE THE OTHER PERSON'S FEELINGS IN THE WAY YOU WORD YOUR APOLOGY.

EXPLAIN HOW YOU WILL PUT THINGS RIGHT

MAKING AMENDS

Your apology should incorporate your intention to restore trust in the relationship. Include the specifics of how you will make things right between you. Although this point has been touched on previously, it is worth exploring more fully.

For example, if you borrowed your brother-in-law's lawn mower and broke it, then you need to pay to get it fixed, making the arrangements to drop it off at a repair facility, pick it up when it is ready, and deliver it to your brother-in-law's house.

Or, to build on the illustration from the previous chapter of the brother who failed to pay back the loan, if you borrowed money from a family member and neglected to repay it, you need to express heartfelt regret to the person, along with a realistic plan to pay back the money. If you know that paying it back completely within a short period of time would likely be impossible, then let the person know your finances have become tight or you misjudged the income you would have available. Be sure to tell them your circumstances and reasons so they can understand your perspective.

Remember that the important aspect of making things right is to present a plan that will reestablish genuine trust with the other person. That is why, instead of promising that all the money will be paid back within a short time, you need to be truthful and realistic. People are more likely to be understanding when you are honest and making your very best effort to correct the situation. For instance, you might offer to make installment payments every week for the next four weeks until the debt is paid in full. Most of all, convey your regret for the harm you have caused and your intention to make things right as soon as you can.

Making things right says a great deal about your integrity. If you say you are sorry without making any effort to rectify the situation, then any words of apology will come across as weak and meaningless—because they will be. And your reputation will suffer in the long run. If you don't make things right, not only will your relationship become strained but your character will be scarred. Your behavior, including the act of apologizing and making restitution, is your responsibility. God will hold you accountable for your own actions, not someone else's.

**PROPER APOLOGIES HAVE THREE PARTS:
(1) WHAT I DID WAS WRONG.
(2) I FEEL BAD THAT I HURT YOU.
(3) HOW DO I MAKE THIS BETTER?**
—RANDY PAUSCH, AUTHOR AND SCIENTIST

I am not saying all of this to alarm you. I am trying to make you aware of the reality of the consequences of your decisions and actions. God sees all that you do, and He wants you to be obedient to Him. This includes apologizing when you have wronged someone and seeking to make amends, as we are told to do in Scripture.

Make every effort to live in peace with everyone and to be holy; without holiness no one will see the Lord. (Hebrews 12:14)

Putting things right is in your best interest. Again, making reparations following an apology is what keeps your reputation in good standing and may improve the way others perceive your character.

COMMITTING TO NOT DO IT AGAIN

Apologizing also means that you are making a commitment to not offend the person in that way ever again. In most instances, the person needs to hear you say those words. It can have a tremendous effect on healing the relationship. Bring up the issue in a nonconfrontational manner and express your interest in making the relationship better. If the other person reacts poorly to what you are saying, then let it go.

There are some situations where making things right has more to do with your behavior moving forward than making reparations. For example, if you have been unfaithful in your marriage, you can't go back and undo the sin you committed. However, you can make a promise to never be unfaithful again. You can commit to going to counseling with your spouse to work through the hurt and brokenness. You can also change other behavioral patterns as part of your sincere apology. If you cheated with someone whom you met on social media, your reparations for the infidelity might include deleting your social media accounts or providing your spouse with all passwords and full transparency regarding your online activity.

Perhaps you haven't committed adultery but are emotionally abusive to your spouse. You have repeatedly apologized and said you would change, but this has not happened. In your heart, you may want to change, but every time you get into an argument, you become so enraged you cannot hold back the name-calling, belittling, and insults. You regret your words every time you say them, but in the heat of the moment, you don't know how to stop yourself. The result has been years of emotional abuse that your spouse can no longer endure. Your promises are empty words, and your spouse is now seriously contemplating filing for divorce.

It is not always easy to make a commitment to change and then follow through with that decision. Often, we can't make lasting changes without help from outside sources. If you are in a situation similar to the ones just described, do yourself and your relationships a favor by seeking out resources that can help you. If you don't know how to make the changes happen in your behavior and life, then you will not be successful. Understanding the steps involved and the kind of commitment necessary will enable you to start on a positive path toward transformation.

You can do an online search or obtain recommendations from trusted individuals to identify support groups that can assist you with your efforts to alter your behavior. Join a group and commit to it so you can learn from others what helped them make lasting changes in their lives. Going to a counselor or therapist can also help you make real transformation happen. A book, magazine article, or blog about the topic might also enable you to better understand your own behavior and learn how to begin to make changes.

Get the help you need before all your significant relationships are destroyed. You never know when your spouse or another family member will have reached their limit. Your next indiscretion, argument, or abusive episode might be the final straw. Don't let it get to that point. Turn the situation over to God for His guidance and strength and find the professional assistance you need. All things are possible when you seek God's help in your situation.

For I can do everything through Christ, who gives me strength.
(Philippians 4:13 NLT)

A commitment to change is a wonderful decision when it leads you to improve yourself and heal and strengthen your relationships. What is most important is to follow through with your efforts to make those changes happen. The preservation of your relationships may depend on it.

THE SECRET OF CHANGE IS TO FOCUS ALL OF YOUR ENERGY NOT ON FIGHTING THE OLD, BUT ON BUILDING THE NEW.

—DAN MILLMAN,
WAY OF THE PEACEFUL WARRIOR: A BOOK THAT CHANGES LIVES

CHAPTER RECAP

Apologizing to someone for a wrong you have committed against them is your way of telling them they are important in your life and you want to heal the relationship by acknowledging your wrongdoing. It is also your verbal commitment to righting your wrong.

Some important tips for making an apology include the following: (1) express genuine remorse, (2) check your tone of voice and body language, (3) focus on the hurt *you* caused, not the other person's faults, (4) acknowledge your wrong, and (5) explain how you will put things right by making amends and committing to not do it again.

You don't need to go through the process of changing a negative behavior on your own. Support groups, counselors, therapists, books, articles, and blogs can all help you to understand and change the particular behavior you are struggling with.

QUESTIONS FOR REFLECTION

1. Is there someone in your family to whom you owe an apology? What is the status of your relationship with this person? If there is a strain in your relationship, will you make the effort to restore that relationship, demonstrating your love and obedience to God?

2. When you need to apologize to someone, do you often bring up the other person's faults as a defensive measure? How can you change this practice in the future?

3. In what way(s) will you make amends for a wrong you have committed against someone? What is your plan for reestablishing genuine trust with them?

HIDDEN BEHAVIOR #2:

CRITICISM

4

VIEWING CRITICISM AS A HELPFUL TOOL

None of us escapes criticism in this life, and unfortunately, criticism often occurs in extended families. Our family members are usually easy targets for us to fight with and talk back to. Therefore, we tend to be more critical of each other—or more vocal about it.

How do we react to this criticism? Most of us wouldn't lash out at our boss for giving us a negative appraisal of our most recent project. We would likely listen to what they had to say and work on improving our performance. It's much easier to react negatively to our family members when they criticize us because we know each other better…and we also know how to push one another's buttons.

This section of the book will help you learn how to handle criticism, both as the recipient and the deliverer, so that family relationships aren't damaged. You will be empowered to use the feedback you receive as a tool not only to improve yourself but also to strengthen family interactions because you will no longer feel a need to react negatively to criticism. You have the ability to handle criticism so that it can help you become a better person.

THE EFFECTS OF CRITICISM

However, criticism shouldn't be a regular habit within families because we are supposed to be loving, supportive, and encouraging toward one another. Does criticism help to achieve love and harmony in a family? No, it typically creates the opposite result. Criticism makes people feel hurt and angry, resulting in a divided family.

I have written several articles for Lifehack on the subject of criticism in families. In "6 Big Mistakes That Destroy Family Relationships," I summarized the detrimental effects of criticism and what we can do to show support for our loved ones instead:

> When there is any outpouring of these negative words to a family member, the chasm can grow so great that it can almost seem beyond repair. Any relationship can be resolved with apologies and forgiveness, but the hurt can still remain long after the words are exchanged. Be careful with your words. Remind yourself that as family, you are there to be one another's greatest supporters in life. Tearing down others in the family with words is destructive to the family unit. Keep this old adage in mind: "If you don't have something nice to say, don't say anything at all."
>
> If there are people in your family who use negative words, then set the example and set it strong. Use words that encourage and uplift. Doing so makes you a person whom others want to be around. People don't want to be around those who make them feel bad. They want to be around those who make them feel good about themselves. Help your fellow family members by looking for the positive in each and every person.[9]

REMIND YOURSELF THAT AS FAMILY, YOU ARE THERE TO BE ONE ANOTHER'S GREATEST SUPPORTERS IN LIFE.

There is no magic wand we can wave to cease all criticism within our extended family. There will always be relatives who take it upon themselves to correct the lives of others. Nonetheless, there are healthy ways to deal

9. Dr. Magdalena Battles, "6 Big Mistakes That Destroy Family Relationships," Lifehack, https://www.lifehack.org/453749/6-big-mistakes-that-destroy-family-relationships.

with criticism. In this chapter, we will learn how to view criticism as help-ful feedback for improving our lives, regardless of the motivations of the criticizer.

INSULTS VERSUS CONSTRUCTIVE CRITICISM

As I mentioned in chapter 2, there is a difference between insults and constructive criticism. Sometimes, there is a fine line between them, but they are different creatures.

The verb *insult* is defined as:

1. to treat or speak to insolently or with contemptuous rudeness

2. to affect as an affront; offend or demean

3. *Archaic.* to attack; assault

The purpose of an insult is to inflict harm. The speaker is choosing to attack someone else. Attacking and insulting anyone, especially a family member, is not acceptable behavior. Actually, it is a sin to criticize someone else in an insulting way.

There is one whose rash words are like sword thrusts, but the tongue of the wise brings healing. (Proverbs 12:18 ESV)

Insults are used like swords in battle. They pierce a person's soul, dam-aging them to their core. Our words are supposed to be wise, kind, and loving. If we want good relationships, we need to remember that insults should never be part of the family environment.

There are various types of insults, and most slights between family members aren't direct verbal jabs. Instead, they come in the form of sarcas-tic remarks, innuendos, backhanded compliments, and negative nonverbal communications, such as the eye roll. None of these behaviors is helpful for creating healthy family dynamics.

It is *intention* that differentiates criticism from insults. While an insult is lobbed with the purpose of harming, criticism is given with the purpose of helping. However, even criticism that is offered with good intentions can have the effect of an insult if it is badly expressed. When this happens, positive relationships are undermined. Yet when constructive criticism is delivered and received in a healthy manner, it can help to build up individual family members and their relationships at the same time.

OVERLY CRITICAL PEOPLE ARE AVOIDED

When someone is habitually bombarded by criticism, they don't want to be around whoever is criticizing them. Avoiding people who are habitually critical of us is a form of self-preservation. Imagine this scenario:

Brother to you: "Wow, your lasagna recipe is the same as it was ten years ago. Maybe you should try something new next time."

Sister to you: "You need help in choosing clothing that actually looks good for your shape because that outfit is not the most flattering on you."

Dad to you: "Your husband tells the worst jokes."

Sister to you: "Gosh, at what age do you think you will finally get little Suzy potty-trained? I wonder if there is something wrong with her. Have you asked her doctor about it?"

Mom to you: "Oh, it looks like that diet didn't work for you. How long did you actually stick to it?"

Everyone in your family to you: *"Why don't you want to spend time with us?"*

When we are constantly the recipient of disapproving words from our family members, our desire to spend time with them will obviously diminish. Relationships will be broken. Unity will be weakened. This is a major reason why both the criticized and the criticizer need practical tips and tools to get a better handle on dealing with the hidden behavior of criticism.

HOW TO MAKE CRITICISM WORK FOR YOU

Family members often hand out criticism because they love us and want to see us live better and more successful lives. However, our human nature often perceives their words as an affront instead of constructive advice. The motivation of the person, the truth behind the message, the delivery, and our personality all play into how we interpret and receive the criticism.

Some people naturally accept criticism as an opportunity to gain insight into themselves and improve, while others are highly sensitive and take it as a judgment that they are not good enough. Being of the former persuasion rather than the latter will help you profitably receive and process input from your family members and foster better family relationships. You will be more likely to accept the information if you see it as an indication that your loved ones care enough about you to help correct a wrong attitude or counterproductive behavior. If you only look at the criticism as judgment, then you will likely become defensive and even verbally strike back.

Understanding how to process criticism appropriately provides you with occasions to develop both personally and professionally. Friend, it is crucial to view all criticism from this fresh angle so you can react in an emotionally intelligent manner. Regardless of your personality, you can teach yourself to view these experiences as opportunities rather than threats. Ultimately, you will benefit if you decide not to wallow in self-pity, feelings of inadequacy, or defeatism. Let's look at several tips for how to make criticism work for you.

LOOK FOR THE TRUTH IN WHAT THE OTHER PERSON IS SAYING

You may not agree with everything someone says about you, but consider whether a small bit of what they are saying is true. Being willing to acknowledge that small truth can lead you to do some honest introspection outside of your conversation with them. Use the situation to process the information and learn how to accept some of what they are saying while shrugging off the rest.

Proverbs 10:17 says, "*Whoever heeds discipline shows the way to life, but whoever ignores correction leads others astray.*" If you can identify something to improve or change, the next step is simply to make a plan to do it. Self-improvement books on almost every subject under the sun are available online, in bookstores, or in libraries. Use the Internet to look for other resources that can help your self-improvement efforts.

Don't expect to change in one day! Change is a process. Take one step at a time, one day at a time, and make the transformation happen. Ultimately, do it for yourself, not because a family member pointed out your flaws.

PROGRESS IS IMPOSSIBLE WITHOUT CHANGE, AND THOSE WHO CANNOT CHANGE THEIR MINDS CANNOT CHANGE ANYTHING.
—GEORGE BERNARD SHAW

For example, imagine you have a gap between your front teeth and your cousin often likes to ask when you are going to "get that fixed." You can decide whether you like having the gap. Some people enjoy being different. If you want a gap between your front teeth because it makes you distinctly you, then embrace it. The next time your cousin says something about it, you can thank them for their concern but let them know you like the way it looks and don't feel a need to change it. However, if you determine that the gap bothers you, also, then choose to make a change. Schedule an appointment with a dentist and go from there. Even if you think you wouldn't want to wear braces or can't afford orthodontic work, know your options before you rule out a decision to make a modification.

Again, it's important not to allow criticism from another person to dictate changes in your life. However, don't rule out self-improvement and change just because you don't like to hear negative things about yourself. When you receive criticism, put it in your back pocket. When you're ready, consider the advice and decide for yourself what you want to do.

MOVE FORWARD IF THERE IS NO BASIS FOR THE CRITICISM

There are some instances when the criticism has no basis whatsoever. Even at those times, you can express gratitude for the feedback and then move forward. To use a simple example, suppose your daughter doesn't like it when you wear the color black. She would rather that you wear pink all the time, so every time you wear black, she complains about it to you. Her opinion about this isn't really relevant in the scheme of your life, so you can thank her for her input but explain that you will wear what you feel is necessary for that day.

You don't need to stay in a conversation in which both parties differ in their opinions so much that a middle ground will never be found. If the criticizer insists you need to change, but you have assessed the situation and determined they are incorrect in their evaluation, resist the temptation to linger and argue about *how* you are right. Some people will never concede their point, regardless of proof or logic to the contrary. Accepting that fact will help you move forward and not be influenced by people who can't see the reality of a situation.

I once wrote an article for my blog on the theme of fashion style, and one woman who replied to my post called me shallow. She ranted that the topic of fashion was not meaningful. I write about a lot of subjects, some serious, some more lighthearted. I appreciate style and enjoy dressing up, but that isn't the basis of who I am as a person. This woman's comments made me feel that I shouldn't ever discuss fashion.

I realized that I could "show her," but I didn't want to spend more than a minute or two responding to her rant. I could have simply deleted her reply (and her online presence on my blog), but I didn't. Rather than reacting in anger or dismissiveness, I responded with love and kindness. I provided a link to a recent article I had written about helping others and giving back. I also let her know that she could browse my website and find lots of other articles that she would perhaps find meaningful. She replied, "Thank you. I will check these articles out."

I receive feedback on lots of my articles, mostly good, but some not so good. I have learned to take this criticism in stride. Sometimes, I acknowledge there is a point to what people are saying that is worth hearing. The assessment of the woman who judged my character and life purpose based on one article about fashion was inaccurate, and it was also not how I saw myself. A short answer that disproved her erroneous idea of me diffused her criticism. I was able to clarify that she misunderstood who I am and what I am about. I defended myself but did so with kindness. Of course, my initial reaction was hurt, and a few choice words probably crossed my mind. However, the way I ultimately reacted and what I wrote in response was proof of my character at that moment in time.

Being criticized is a frequent experience for most of us. We can learn not to take it personally by knowing who we are. This point is vital because experiencing the judgment of others when you don't yet know your own value can cause you to personalize their opinions, making them your own. Don't allow that to happen. Stand firm in the fact that God created you to be you. It may be your life purpose to be a fashion blogger. God gave you a gift and a vision. Great, embrace it and be who He made you to be! Carry on with your work and let the naysayers continue to criticize. Don't feed their criticism by responding to it in a way that allows them to diminish who you are as a person or the vision God has given you. Love what you do because you were created for that purpose.

Learning to take criticism as a suggestion, one that you can take or leave, empowers you to decide what is best for your own life. This makes criticism easier to hear and filter through your own personal value system. So move past undue criticism. In life, if you are good at anything and become successful, you will endure criticism. A life that isn't criticized is likely a life that is not influencing anyone. The greater the number of people you influence and affect, the more you open yourself to the opinions of others. It will be difficult for you to remain successful if you don't know how to handle criticism properly. And interactions with our family members are great opportunities for learning how to receive criticism and process it maturely.

LEARNING TO TAKE CRITICISM AS A SUGGESTION, ONE THAT YOU CAN TAKE OR LEAVE, EMPOWERS YOU TO DECIDE WHAT IS BEST FOR YOUR OWN LIFE.

PRACTICE HEARING WITHOUT OVERREACTING

Another tip for making criticism work for you is to practice hearing it without overreacting. In this way, unsolicited advice from a family member can turn into an occasion for learning to become a good listener. Think of the experience as training for other everyday situations at home, at work, or with friends. As you are being criticized, you might be mentally discrediting what the other person is saying and defending yourself, but you do not need to get into a heated discussion with them about your thoughts. You can choose not to be combative about receiving the critique.

Imagine you are at a family Christmas gathering and your aunt says, "You should think about growing out your hair. Men like long hair, and you would make yourself more appealing in the dating pool." Ouch, that stings! You weren't looking for any input from her about your hair or your dating life.

However, you can practice this new concept of receiving criticism without overreacting by listening and responding with kindness rather than rudeness or condescension. Proverbs 15:1 tells us, *"A gentle answer turns away wrath, but a harsh word stirs up anger."* Perhaps your initial thought was to say, "My dating life is none of your business, and I like my hair the way it is!" This reaction would not foster kindness or love in your relationship with your aunt. Instead, you might thank her by saying something like, "I appreciate your concern about my dating life, but I am really focused on finishing my law degree. It's good food for thought, though, when I have time to begin dating again." By showing your aunt that you listened to her opinion and communicating that you are not interested in dating right now, she can better understand your viewpoint and priorities. Holding back your initial response to the criticism will enable your relationship to be maintained and even grow. Best of all, she will feel appreciated that you listened to her perspective.

You can also provide feedback to the criticizer in a manner that creates better communication for the future. Someone may have said something critical to you that was valid, but their delivery really put you off. You can say to the person, "You do have some good points, but it would help me if you would not raise your voice while telling me your concerns." This is an opportunity to assist the other person in learning better ways of communicating with you, while still taking their points into consideration.

It is also a good practice to filter the message that comes through a bad delivery. It is easier to take criticism when it is said calmly and kindly, but this won't always happen. Practice in accepting criticism that is true but harshly delivered will further empower you to become a better listener with an ability to wade through the junk to the actual message.

WHEN SOMEONE IS RIGHT, DEMONSTRATE MATURITY BY VERBALLY ACKNOWLEDGING IT

If there is some truth in what your family member is saying, acknowledging that truth is not a weakness. It takes a strong individual to be able to recognize a fault and willingly say, "Yes, you are probably right." For example, if your mother points out that you promised to help with the Thanksgiving meal but then forgot to follow through, then accept responsibility. Apologize and offer to make things right. It is emotionally mature to acknowledge and accept that you did something wrong and admit that you need to improve. It also demonstrates your willingness to pursue personal growth. If the information your family member gave you can help you change and become a better version of yourself, then remember to thank them. *"Oil and perfume make the heart glad, and the sweetness of a friend comes from his earnest counsel"* (Proverbs 27:9 ESV).

CREATE AN OCCASION FOR FEEDBACK AND HELP

If you acknowledge you have a problem or fault and desire to fix it, it is often beneficial to put the ball back in the criticizer's court, asking, "What would you do about this if it were you?" Make them personalize the problem so they can put themselves in your shoes. Asking them in this manner will help them see things from your perspective and make them think more realistically about solutions.

When you open the door to meaningful conversations by asking what a family member would do if they were in your situation, you may find that your criticizer has some helpful suggestions that you would have missed out on if you had brushed off their advice, argued with them about it, or reacted defensively. Most of the time, when we accept criticism from a family member who is motivated by love and concern, it results in our receiving help in finding solutions. Keep in mind that true care between family members does not just mean pointing out people's problems but also being a part of remedying them.

Suppose your extended family is gathered at your parents' home for the Thanksgiving holiday weekend. You have come with your spouse and children, and your siblings have come with their families. Over dinner one evening, your sister-in-law points out that your sixteen-month-old son shouldn't be gagging so much while he is eating. Your son refuses to eat pureed food, and you have cut up his meal into the tiniest pieces possible. You feel like you are doing everything you can to enable your child to eat, but your sister-in-law's comment and tone make you feel like she is criticizing you as a mother.

Rather than getting annoyed at her, you can ask kindly, "What would you recommend? I can't make the pieces any smaller and he won't eat mushy food." She responds by telling you about the swallow study her daughter participated in when she was a baby, which came by way of a referral from their pediatrician to a specialist. It turns out your niece also had problems with swallowing as a baby.

You didn't even know there was such a thing as a swallow study! If you hadn't asked for her advice but instead responded with a verbal jab, the conversation would have been shut down and you would not have heard about the study and specialist. You created a learning opportunity and found help for your child by simply asking your sister-in-law what she would do in this situation. It may not have been easy to ask for her opinion because you initially felt insulted, but it certainly showed emotional maturity. It was also an opportunity to stretch and build your criticism-taking muscles.

> EVERY HUMAN BEING IS ENTITLED TO COURTESY AND CONSIDERATION. CONSTRUCTIVE CRITICISM IS NOT ONLY TO BE EXPECTED BUT SOUGHT.
> —MARGARET CHASE SMITH, FIRST WOMAN TO SERVE IN BOTH HOUSES OF THE U.S. CONGRESS

TAKE THE OPPORTUNITY TO STRENGTHEN RELATIONSHIPS

Having your family member look at your problem as their problem creates an occasion for bonding that can strengthen and deepen your relationship. For example, I have two brothers who were adopted from Peru. One of my brothers was contacted through social media by some individuals in his native country who claimed to be his biological siblings. My brother was interested in meeting them, but his wife was concerned about how he was handling this contact from his potential family members. I had some concerns, too, and tried to express them in a manner that wasn't overly critical. I certainly didn't want to prevent him from finding his biological family. I just wanted to make sure he was acting safely, especially if he was planning to meet these individuals in person. My concern was that he might be conned by people in a foreign country who were not actually related to him.

Of course, being an older sister, I don't always express my criticism well when speaking to my younger siblings! However, my brother turned things around, asking how I would handle the situation if it were me. It made me really think and prompted me to do some online research about DNA testing abroad. I provided this information to my brother, and then it was up to him whether he wanted to use it.

Through this process, our relationship was strengthened because we now shared a connection in his search for his biological family. He pursued the DNA testing and discovered that the people who had contacted him were indeed his relatives. He even invited me to come along and meet them in Peru when he and his wife traveled there. Unfortunately, because I have three small children, I was unable to go. However, I was thrilled for him, delighted in seeing his photos, and rejoiced in the stories he told about meeting his new family members.

My brother and I bonded over a sensitive subject in a situation that could have turned ugly if we had not been respectful and loving toward one another. He invited me into the process by asking me to put myself in his shoes, and it worked! I placed myself in his circumstances and was willing to help be part of the solution. Our brother-sister relationship became deeper because of a difficult conversation that began with criticism.

RESPOND WITH PEACE INSTEAD OF HOSTILITY

By reacting positively when criticism comes your way, you can also be a peacemaker in your family. Remember that a positive reaction involves expressing appreciation for the person's concern while processing the information as you deem right. You may choose to disregard the criticism and explain your perspective, or you may find some truth in it and make a plan to change, including asking for help in creating a solution. When you react in either of these ways, you are choosing harmony over hostility. You might be tempted to blame the criticizer for stirring up conflict, but in reality, it is your response that will inflame or diffuse the situation. Nobody can force you to react poorly—you make that choice yourself. When you choose peace, you are taking the high road and developing better character.

Imagine you are at a family dinner following your daughter's dance recital. Your brother remarks, out of the children's hearing, that the performance was great but would have been better if your daughter hadn't made the mistake of turning in the wrong direction, breaking formation with the other dancers.

It is not really that big of a deal since your daughter is only seven years old, but the criticism feels completely uncalled for in this setting. You might start to become defensive and want to tell your brother that his children aren't perfect either. But rather than initiating World War III by reminding him that his ten-year-old caused his entire baseball team to lose their playoff game last season because he struck out, you hold back. You choose peace over anger and hostility and simply state, "No, Anna is not perfect, but we are so proud that she did her best." This peaceful response will help him to see the positive in the situation as well. The fact is, it was a delightful overall performance. And truly, nobody is perfect.

He answers by saying, "You're right; it was a very good recital and she did great." Your decision to respond in a manner that is calm and doesn't create hostility is an emotionally mature choice. Pointing out his child's fault would only have provoked your brother. Even though he just criticized your child, you rose above it. You chose to be an example and you maintained peace in the family. Over time, as you convey other positive reactions and actions, you will build an atmosphere in which there is less family criticism and hostility. Some of those positive reactions and actions include providing praise and compliments to your loved ones and being a helper, supporter, and encourager. *"Blessed are the peacemakers, for they will be called children of God"* (Matthew 5:9).

CHOOSE SELF-RESPECT

We all have faults, so acknowledging them shouldn't be that hard. But as we know, when someone points them out to us, our gut reaction is to disagree, argue, or retaliate with a verbal jab. Yet whenever we choose not to react negatively, we choose self-respect. Additionally, we gain respect from others who are wise enough to recognize our mature response.

As I wrote in chapter 1, when my husband and I got married, we became pregnant with our first child right away. When I was about four months along, we went to visit family, and I was proud to be wearing my first maternity blouse. I was finally beginning to develop a pregnant belly! It was a joyful time for my husband and me.

Then, a family member commented that my maternity blouse wasn't flattering. They said I didn't look pregnant but instead just looked like I was getting fat. I was hurt by this comment, but in the spirit of giving family members the benefit of the doubt, I chose not to react emotionally. I wanted to tell this person they weren't a model of fitness themselves. However, I knew that a tit-for-tat approach in situations where criticism is expressed merely leads to insults.

Instead, I responded by saying, "Oh, really? I guess I won't wear this blouse again" and laughed it off. I made the situation lighthearted (but never did wear that blouse a second time!). After we left that day, my husband shared his thoughts on the conversation. He said I had given a very kind and mature response. He also said I looked great! And he pointed out that this family member doesn't think before they speak and often has foot-in-mouth syndrome.

Thank goodness my husband hadn't been able to read my thoughts at the time the criticism was spoken! In order to maintain harmony, I had made a decision not to respond to the comment in a harsh way. In doing so, I gained additional respect from my husband and diffused a potential conflict with a family member. I am grateful I chose my words in kindness rather than reacting with hurt and anger. Who knows? Maybe this person likes to test people's character by seeing if they can induce a negative reaction. It was up to me how I chose to react that day, and that is still the case. Every time there is an occasion when we see this family member, I make a choice about how I will react to them. I also choose how much time I spend in their company.

I have since discovered that although this person often speaks without thinking, they can be very sensitive to how people treat them. I would likely have damaged the relationship if I had reacted poorly to the first criticism I received from them. And I have learned to take their comments with a grain of salt. Some people just lack a filter. Do you know anyone like that? You can gain respect from others by recognizing this personality type and responding in kindness rather than anger. We need to think about the comments we are about to make, decide if they are wise, and commit to speaking only positive words.

Choosing self-respect is part of the process of making yourself more open to hearing and processing criticism. Being able to take criticism makes you more efficient at identifying and accepting the messages that are valid. This saves you time while empowering you to disregard opinions that are of no real use to you. When I was younger, I competed in the Miss America scholarship pageant system, which helped me pay for a great deal of my education for my undergraduate and master's degrees. When I advanced to the state level after having won a regional title, I was assigned a committee that was to assist me in preparing for that competition. This committee gave me lots of great advice—from whitening my teeth to writing a better resume. Most of the suggestions were very useful and I applied them to my pageant planning.

However, one member of the committee suggested that I cut my long hair to make me look more professional and "polished." I valued my long hair. It was part of what I liked about myself at that time in my life, so I thanked the person for their input but said I would not be cutting my hair. Other young women at the national level of competition had long hair like mine, and I determined that it was merely an opinion that my hair didn't look polished.

I found out later that others on the committee thought it would be a shame if I cut my hair, and they agreed with my defense. They just didn't want to say anything during the committee discussion that would undermine a fellow leader on the team. While the committee provided excellent advice as a whole and I listened to all of it, that didn't mean I needed to apply every aspect of it to my pageant preparations.

Again, knowing who you were created to be helps you process the opinions of others and respond to them in a way that affirms your self-respect. Don't dwell on irrelevant criticism. You can learn to listen, make a choice, and then move forward as you become more willing to hear with an open mind.

BEING ABLE TO TAKE CRITICISM MAKES YOU MORE EFFICIENT AT IDENTIFYING AND ACCEPTING THE MESSAGES THAT ARE VALID.

WHEN THE SAME BASELESS CRITICISM KEEPS COMING UP, ADDRESS THE ISSUE DIRECTLY

What should you do if the same baseless criticism keeps surfacing? Suppose you have a few family members who continually make comments about your weight. They are very health-conscious and think you are not as fit as they are and therefore are unhealthy. According to your doctor, your health is just fine, and you are tired of hearing these family members repeatedly criticize you.

Instead of waiting for the next time they bring up the topic, address the issue yourself. Doing so will help you not to react to their criticism defensively or harshly, which could negatively affect your relationship with them. Take each person aside separately and talk to them. First, acknowledge that you know they say these things out of love and concern for you. Show them you hear what they are saying and understand their point of view.

Next, tell them what your doctor says and express that you no longer want them to bring up this subject. Speak firmly but kindly, keeping in mind that their motivation is their concern for you. You might say, "I respect and appreciate your opinion on this matter, but we do not need to discuss it again. Please do not bring it up in the future." Such conversations are not easy to have, but they do let the other person know how you feel about the comments they have been making. They show you feel strongly about not hearing those remarks anymore and are taking the time to have an honest conversation to address the topic.

Once you have had these conversations, consider the issue closed. If a family member "forgets," simply remind them in a friendly and kind tone.

For example, you might say, "Remember the conversation we had about this topic?" That should be enough for them to stop talking about the subject. However, if they continue, you have the right to shut down the conversation. Walking away is the best way to convey that you are serious about not discussing it any longer.

THE FINAL PROOF OF GREATNESS LIES IN BEING ABLE TO ENDURE CRITICISM WITHOUT RESENTMENT.
—ELBERT HUBBARD, WRITER AND PUBLISHER

CHAPTER RECAP

When criticism between family members is delivered improperly, it is perceived as an insult, which does nothing to foster good family relationships. The goal is to keep criticism to a minimum. Instead of criticizing our family members, we should uplift, encourage, and support them. That is what love within a family is all about.

Although insults between family members are never acceptable, there are healthy ways in which criticism can be handled and filtered by the receiver. Tips for making criticism work for you include the following: look for the truth in what the person is saying; move forward if there is no basis for the criticism; practice hearing without overreacting; when someone is right, demonstrate maturity by verbally acknowledging it; create an occasion for feedback and help; take the opportunity to strengthen relationships; respond with peace instead of hostility; choose self-respect; and when the same baseless criticism keeps coming up, address the issue directly.

QUESTIONS FOR REFLECTION

1. Do your family members often criticize one another? Or, do you have one family member in particular who is prone to criticize others?

2. How would you describe the way criticism is given and received in your family?

3. In what ways do you usually respond to criticism from your family members? How can you respond in more constructive ways?

5

HOW TO OFFER CONSTRUCTIVE CRITICISM

Clearly, nobody wants to be around someone who makes them feel bad about themselves. That is why those who make a habit of being critical of their family members must understand they are putting their relationships in jeopardy. In my own family, I have sometimes been guilty of being overly critical, and it has even caused my own small children to avoid me!

For example, when my kids were helping me in the kitchen the other day, I was in a generally irritated mood already, so every action around me seemed like the equivalent of fingernails being scraped across a blackboard. One of my twins was unloading the dishwasher and stacking plates in this fashion: small, large, small, large. I became annoyed because the plates go in separate stacks in the cabinet, one for small plates and the other for large plates. I told him this and then said, "You know better; you have been doing this for a while now."

My daughter was setting the table at the same time and her actions sounded obnoxiously loud to me. My reaction to her was, "Can't you do that more quietly? You are so loud when you set the table. It doesn't need to be that loud." Of course, when I made those statements, my tone was not the nicest.

I also noted that my other son was not putting away the school shoes fast enough. Plus, he was putting them on the wrong shelves. I let him know the mistakes he was making, too, and I didn't sugarcoat the message.

All the kids clammed up, got their work done, and ran out of the kitchen as fast as they could. They didn't want to be around me. They knew I was in a foul mood and was ready to pounce on their every action.

I was wrong in my words and my behavior. I was wrong in the tone I used and the way I corrected them. I really didn't need to correct them at all. They were getting their jobs done. It might not have been the way I would have done it, but what did that matter if the tasks were completed?

DOES YOUR FAMILY WANT TO BE AROUND YOU?

In our extended families, we often criticize one another because we each have different ways of doing things that we think are better than everyone else's and we want to convey this information. We care about our loved ones and see their potential, so our intention is to help them. The problem is usually our delivery. We end up using tones that insult people, causing our messages to go in one ear and out the other. They don't want to listen when we act judgmental or insulting toward them because it makes them feel unappreciated and put upon. They want to get far away from us, just like my children did with me. Don't make yourself the outcast of the family by being unnecessarily critical or delivering criticism in a manner that comes off as judgmental or insulting. The criticism should be carried out in a constructive way; hence the term *constructive criticism*.

When people get together at family gatherings, they want to feel happy and uplifted as they connect with their relatives. Family time should mean enjoying being with one another and creating shared life experiences. If someone uses that opportunity to point out the flaws of others, they diminish the happiness of the gathering, and their connection with family members becomes more difficult. It's hard to have relationships with people when you feel they are always looking for your faults.

BE AN ENCOURAGER.
THE WORLD HAS PLENTY OF CRITICS ALREADY.
—DAVE WILLIS, PASTOR AND WRITER

"WHAT IS THE UPSIDE OF SAYING THIS?"

When it comes to sharing our opinions, we must ask ourselves the following question before opening our mouth to speak: "What is the upside of saying this?" If there is no upside and the criticism is only going to inflict pain or cause the other party to become upset, then we don't need to say it. For example, telling your daughter she has awful taste in clothing is *not* worth expressing. You are only going to hurt her feelings and damage the relationship. To merely point out a fault or flaw is not helpful. If you have a genuine concern, such as, you think her clothing is inappropriate for her job and may hinder her success there, then address the issue with that specific concern in mind and offer to go shopping with her or gift her with some better clothing options.

Keep in mind that because people in families share a bond, they mistakenly think they have permission to say whatever is on their mind, regardless of the hurt it may inflict. But if you filter your messages through the question "What is the upside of saying this?" you can determine if the comment is a blanket criticism without a solution or will truly help the person.

A GENERAL POLICY BETWEEN IN-LAWS TO FOSTER POSITIVE RELATIONSHIPS

People tend to be more sensitive to criticism from their in-laws, so we should not offer it to those who have married into the family. It is generally a good policy to steer clear of critiques and advice unless they are asked for by these individuals. My mother-in-law provided a great example of how to do this in the right way.

When I married my husband, his two siblings had been married for several years and each of them had two children, so my mother-in-law was seasoned in the mother and daughter-in-law relationship. She admitted to me that she had made mistakes in the past, but she had learned from those errors. She told me she would never offer criticism or advice unless it was solicited. For seven years before she passed away, she kept her word. We had a good relationship because of the healthy boundaries she established. I did ask her advice about my children when they were babies, and she was always helpful and happy that I had asked for her input.

Another promise she made was never to drop by our house without first calling to ask if she could come over. This was especially significant because we lived just one street away from my in-laws for the first four years of our marriage. My mother-in-law never did drop by unannounced, even though she went past our house almost every day during her morning walks. She always called and asked if she could stop by, and I don't remember ever saying no. I appreciated the courtesy of the call, which gave me the opportunity to pick up the house quickly if it didn't look presentable or take off my pj's and throw on an outfit if it was already past noon. Simple courtesies go a long way toward making a relationship pleasant and loving.

This policy of not giving unsolicited advice should extend to all in-law relationships, including sisters-in-law and brothers-in-law. It will help to keep relationships friendly and kind. There is no need to nitpick those who have married into the family. For some reason, many families set a precedent in which in-laws are subject to increased criticism. Such behavior makes family gatherings uncomfortable, tense, and even loathsome.

If you want to create a family that is fun, loving, and accepting, then you need to establish a general policy that those who have married into the family are to be treated with respect and gentleness. They are guests in the family, and you wouldn't treat other guests in your home with criticism and negativity, so please don't do that to those who have joined your family through marriage.

SIMPLE COURTESIES GO A LONG WAY TOWARD MAKING A RELATIONSHIP PLEASANT AND LOVING.

OFFERING CONSTRUCTIVE CRITICISM

Criticism should not be expressed between family members unless it is absolutely necessary. But remember that while insults are never helpful in a family, there is a time and place for constructive criticism. There are ways criticizers can improve their delivery when bringing up problems so they can shift from hurting others to uplifting them. Here are some methods for discussing difficult or sensitive issues with family members using empathy and kindness.

BE GENTLE AND SOLUTION-ORIENTED

The book of Galatians provides clear direction on how to approach someone when correcting them:

> *Brothers, if anyone is caught in any transgression, you who are spiritual should restore him in a spirit of gentleness. Keep watch on yourself, lest you too be tempted. Bear one another's burdens, and so fulfill the law of Christ.* (Galatians 6:1–2 ESV)

If you are going to have a talk with a family member because there is something wrong in their life that needs to be corrected, whether it is a sin or a misjudgment, then you need to do so with gentleness and kindness. You also had better have a great solution in mind and be willing to help bear their burden in overcoming this fault. If you don't have a solution and aren't committed to helping the person, then don't bother telling them what is wrong in the first place. It is crucial to be solution-oriented if you are to effectively and lovingly utilize criticism with your fellow family members. (In the next section, we will explore in more detail what it means to bear another person's burden.)

Ask God to give you wisdom for the best way to deliver the message gently and help bear the burden alongside the individual. James 3:17 tells us, "*But the wisdom that comes from heaven is first of all pure; then peace-loving, considerate, submissive, full of mercy and good fruit, impartial and sincere.*"

IF YOUR CRITIQUE SIMPLY REPRESENTS A DIFFERENT WAY OF DOING THINGS, THEN THE CRITICISM OR CORRECTION IS NOT NEEDED.

Keep in mind that if your critique is not about a sin or another harmful behavior but simply represents a different way of doing things, then it is not needed. We are all unique people with very different ways of doing things. Even if you believe your way is better, that doesn't mean you need to correct your family member. It will likely only hurt their feelings. Our family members' personalities may bother or irritate us, but it is important to decide whether their behavior hurts themselves or others...or is just different.

HELP BEAR THE BURDEN

Let me emphasize again, kind reader, not to provide criticism or correction unless you can and *will* help the person to overcome their fault or understand their error. Simply telling someone they need to change is not the same as helping to carry their burden. If you only judge or criticize, you will just make the person feel bad and harm your relationship with them.

Bearing a burden with a family member or fellow Christian means to walk with them as they work to correct thoughts and behaviors that are unproductive, harmful, and rooted in sin. This includes praying with them, praying for them in your own quiet time, and continuing to meet with them in person or by other means until they have overcome their problem. Different issues will require different levels of burden-bearing.

One of my sisters, Natalie, went through a rough time several years ago. She had experienced a difficult breakup and was recovering from serving as a military guard at Guantanamo Bay. Another sister, Rachel, reached out to help her get back on the right track. Rachel also discussed some tough topics with Natalie. Her words were gentle and loving, communicating a true desire to help. The assistance Rachel and her husband provided lasted for several years and included opening their home to Natalie.

Natalie turned her life around and thrived during those years. She finished her undergraduate degree and found a great job. I certainly don't want to refer to my sister as a "burden," but Rachel and my brother-in-law did make a substantial personal and financial commitment during that time, providing Natalie with housing, food, and other necessities. They chose to go above and beyond, but they did so because they loved her and wanted to help. They did not just give her money and hope she would overcome her obstacles. No, they invited her to be part of their family so they could mentor and guide her.

Through the actions of Rachel and her husband, Natalie was enabled to change her life. *This* is the kind of commitment that serious correction entails. If we aren't willing to help by walking alongside our family members and providing for them in practical ways, then we aren't following what Scripture instructs us to do.

Again, we need to ask God for the best words to discuss our concerns with our loved one, without judging them, and the wisdom to help them overcome their burden. Then, we can provide concrete solutions and bear their burden alongside them. Suppose you have a family member who has a serious problem, such as infidelity or addiction. If you simply tell them what they are doing wrong and you can't or won't assist with the solution, you will only be perceived as a criticizer and meddler. Although you won't be able to personally supply all the assistance they need, you can connect them to the most effective resources. You can research their particular issue and look for practical solutions such as counseling and rehab.

And instead of simply telling a family member who has an addiction, "You need to go to rehab," you can find ways to help them afford the solution by looking for sources that can help provide funding for their treatment or programs that are low cost or free of charge and have proven to be successful. A number of churches and organizations offer infidelity and addiction counseling and treatment plans. Search out the best, most reliable options available to your loved one.

Let me add this caution: if you are dealing with a family member who has a history of violence and is physically abusive, I do not advise confronting that person directly about their wrongdoing. Never put yourself in a situation where you will be at risk of harm. Instead, utilize the help of professionals in the field of domestic violence. Within the United States, you can search for local assistance online by going to the website of The National Resource Center on Domestic Violence at https://nrcdv.org. Again, *never* confront a family member about physical abuse. Bring in professionals who know how to protect everyone involved.

USE THE "FEEDBACK SANDWICH" METHOD

Most great communicators know and use the "feedback sandwich" method of expressing constructive criticism. This method is even used by

Toastmasters, an international nonprofit organization that promotes communication and public-speaking skills.[10] The process involves delivering a criticism in between two positive comments. You begin with a genuine compliment. Be specific about the compliment or it will seem insincere. In the next statement, you offer the criticism gently. You conclude with a third comment that is also complimentary. Make sure all three comments or points you raise are related to one another. The goal is to emphasize the positive in order to soften the blow of the criticism for the receiver.

For example, you want to let your sister know that you don't feel comfortable having her children show your children the music videos they watch on YouTube. You feel that your children are too young to be exposed to the mature content. You can begin by saying, "I like how our children play so well together and your kids include my younger children. Would you ask your kids not to show my kids any YouTube videos, though? My kids are younger and don't watch them yet." Finish the sandwich with another compliment: "I do appreciate how you have raised such sweet and inclusive kids. I know they are just trying to be good cousins. How about if I provide some videos for all of the kids to watch when we are together?"

Do you see how using the feedback sandwich method helps to make the conversation more constructive? These statements are much gentler and will be more effective in producing change than saying, for example, "I would never let *my* kids watch those music videos on YouTube, so your kids better not show them to my kids!" Such a statement comes across as judgmental and demanding.

Ephesians 4:15 says, "*Speaking the truth in love....*" In utilizing the feedback sandwich method, your goal is to include positive statements that enhance the relationship and reinforce goodwill. Making the effort to compliment your family member conveys the message that you care. Softening the criticism as much as possible also demonstrates consideration for the other person's feelings.

Combining the instructions in Galatians 6:1–2 with the feedback sandwich method is essential to correcting a family member in a biblical way. The feedback sandwich process provides criticism in a gentle manner but

---

10. Celestine Chua, "How to Give Constructive Criticism: 6 Helpful Tips," *Personal Excellence*, https://personalexcellence.co/blog/constructive-criticism/.

also allows for the incorporation of burden-bearing. In the previous example, gentle, complimentary words surrounded the criticism and included an offer to provide videos for the kids when they got together. This offer was a way of providing a tangible solution and bearing the burden of implementing an alternate suggestion.

CRITICISM, LIKE RAIN, SHOULD BE GENTLE
ENOUGH TO NOURISH A MAN'S GROWTH
WITHOUT DESTROYING HIS ROOTS.
—FRANK A. CLARK, U.S. CONGRESSMAN AND LAWYER

CHAPTER RECAP

Galatians 6:1–2 provides us with sound biblical advice on how to deliver constructive criticism:

> *Brothers, if anyone is caught in any transgression, you who are spiritual should restore him in a spirit of gentleness. Keep watch on yourself, lest you too be tempted. Bear one another's burdens, and so fulfill the law of Christ.* (ESV)

Criticism should be expressed between family members only when it is absolutely necessary. The one criticizing must do so with gentleness and be prepared to bear the burden to help their loved one through the issue. This approach, combined with the feedback sandwich method, is the most loving and effective way of correcting a family member.

QUESTIONS FOR REFLECTION

1. Have you ever criticized a family member because you thought you had a better way of doing something? Was the issue a true problem or was it really just a matter of preference?

2. In what manner do you usually criticize family members who are behaving in a way you feel is harmful to themselves or others? In what ways could you better offer criticism so that it helps rather than hinders your family relationships?

3. What kinds of boundaries does your family have regarding the criticism of in-laws? If you currently don't have any such boundaries in place, how can you encourage your family to set limits on unsolicited advice and criticism toward in-laws?

HIDDEN BEHAVIOR #3:

GOSSIP

6

WHEN DOES CONVERSATION BECOME GOSSIP?

Gossip can be defined as "idle talk or rumor, especially about the personal or private affairs of others." What does gossip do to a family? In this chapter, we're going to look at some of the destructive results of this hidden behavior and learn how to recognize when conversation has disintegrated into gossip.

WHAT GOSSIP DOES TO A FAMILY

GOSSIP VIOLATES TRUST

When family members gossip about other family members, they are undermining the confidence and trust that is necessary for healthy, strong relationships. It is difficult to rebuild trust after there has been an incident of gossiping. It is especially difficult to rebuild trust when gossip has become a family practice. Although trust can be restored even after gossip has occurred, it is easier and more advantageous to avoid it altogether. Gossip is not only tremendously damaging but it is also unproductive. No one can control or change someone else by talking about them.

WHILE TRUST CAN BE RESTORED EVEN
AFTER GOSSIP HAS OCCURRED,
IT IS EASIER AND MORE ADVANTAGEOUS
TO AVOID GOSSIP ALTOGETHER.

GOSSIP CREATES ANXIETY AND TENSION

Gossip often spreads like wildfire in a family. If an atmosphere of gossip is allowed to develop, people become anxious and wonder what is being said about them. They know that gossip is going on because they have heard it. If someone is willing to talk negatively about other family members to us, then they are more than likely talking about us behind our backs too. The tendency of gossipers is to focus on whoever has the most recent or greatest amount of "dirt" on them to discuss.

GOSSIP PRODUCES CONFLICT

Gossip also creates an atmosphere of conflict and taking sides. People get caught up in the negative talk and act like immature teenagers, enjoying the sharing of secrets that others may not know. When family dynamics shift from positive and relationship-building to negative and drama-building, family unity is weakened.

GOSSIP DISTORTS THE FACTS

Did you ever play the game "telephone" when you were growing up? The game begins when one person whispers a specific message into the ear of the person sitting next to them. That person then repeats what they heard to the next person in line. The message is whispered from one person to another until it reaches the last person in the row. The person at the end then states out loud what they heard. Usually, the message has been misconstrued and miscommunicated along the way, so that the final person's message is nothing like the message that was first passed along.

This is the route gossip often takes. Every person contributes their own personal slant to the story, changing it along the way. They repeat the message in their own words, saying what they believe they heard and using their perception of the "facts." Some people will even exaggerate the story on purpose because they thrive on conflict. Therefore, the story is altered in some way each time it is told.

Because of our fallen human nature and propensity to sin, it is unlikely that the person who is being talked about will be portrayed in a better light as time goes on. Usually, the story gets progressively worse. The result is damage to the person's reputation. Whether the information is true or not, the outcome is still the same.

GOSSIP CAUSES DIVISION

Often, there is an element of divisiveness to gossip. For example, suppose someone in your family says to you, "I heard that Sally borrowed a large amount of money from Uncle Jim to keep her business afloat and never repaid it, yet she just bought a new sports car." Whether you desired to hear this information or not, you now know that Sally is in debt to Uncle Jim and may be making unwise financial choices that are harming other family members. You know that Uncle Jim went through a divorce and is struggling to pay his child support. You feel bad for your uncle and his children, who need that money for basic living expenses. The likelihood that you will view or treat Sally differently than you did in the past has now greatly increased. You have emotionally taken a side. Even if you didn't want to be put into a position of taking sides, this is a natural human reaction, especially if you have a strong emotional tie to a family member.

As a result of the gossip, your relationship with Sally has been negatively affected. And the more this information is passed between family members, the greater the number of people who will side with Uncle Jim and form negative feelings toward Sally. Thus, division in the family will occur. However, there might be another side to the story. Perhaps Sally actually repaid the loan and now her business is thriving, and she leased the new car because she got a great deal. The full truth is not being relayed because people don't know the other side. They haven't heard Sally tell it, nor have they asked her to. Unless Sally knows that misinformation is being spread about her and can defend herself, the gossip will divide the family regardless of the truth.

GOSSIP COMPOUNDS PROBLEMS

Suppose Sally had already repaid the loan, but finally learns that this gossip has taken place. She is going to feel hurt. Knowing that people have passed along incorrect information about her throughout the family without first checking its accuracy will break down her trust in her relationships. The same result might happen even if the information were correct. Further division would probably occur because Sally would likely harbor negative feelings toward those who spread the message and gossiped, and she might act in a defensive way. Do you see how gossip can compound a problem, straining relationships and dividing family members further and further down the line? In some cases, it can completely alienate people from one another.

THOSE WHO FEED ON RUMORS ARE SMALL, SUSPICIOUS SOULS.
—CHARLES SWINDOLL, *GROWING STRONG IN THE SEASONS OF LIFE*

WHEN TALK CROSSES THE LINE INTO GOSSIP

When does talk about people cross the line from simple, friendly conversation into the realm of gossip? Here are some criteria to consider:

+ Does the talk have negative undertones?
+ Does the talk make another person look bad?
+ Is the talk damaging to someone's reputation?
+ Would the person feel bad if they knew what was being said about them?
+ Is this intimate information that the person would not like shared with others?
+ Does the sharing of the information seem to be a rejoicing in the misfortune of others?
+ Is the information substantiated or is it mere rumor?

For a message to be considered gossip, it doesn't need to fulfill all the above criteria. It could fit into just one or two categories. When in doubt as to whether information you are about to convey is gossip, err on the side of caution and say nothing at all.

WHAT DOES SCRIPTURE SAY ABOUT GOSSIP?

Again, the best way to handle any issue is God's way. To appreciate what Scripture says about gossip, it is important to first understand the meaning of the word in the Hebrew language, which is the language of the Old

Testament. The website Got Questions examined the topic of gossip from a biblical perspective and gave this description of the person who gossips:

> The Hebrew word translated "gossip" in the Old Testament is defined as "one who reveals secrets, one who goes about as a tale-bearer or scandal-monger." A gossiper is a person who has privileged information about people and proceeds to reveal that information to those who have no business knowing it.[11]

It is abundantly clear, according to this Hebrew word definition and what we have discussed so far, that gossip is not a desirable activity anywhere, especially in the family. Those who engage in gossip are considered "scandal-mongers." In today's language, that might be translated as "drama creators." Those who participate in gossip want to share secrets about others for the purpose of producing drama and scandal. The information is sometimes false and sometimes factual. Either way, it is considered gossip if it damages a person's reputation.

The book of Proverbs has much to say about gossip, and we will glean from its wisdom throughout the rest of this chapter. Consider this proverb:

> *A perverse person stirs up conflict, and a gossip separates close friends.* (Proverbs 16:28)

Gossip can even damage the relationship between close friends, including friends who are related. If you want the relationships between your family members to be friendly, then gossip needs to stay out of all your interactions.

> *The mouths of fools are their undoing, and their lips are a snare to their very lives. The words of a gossip are like choice morsels; they go down to the inmost parts.* (Proverbs 18:7–8)

This passage tells us that gossip is foolish talk. It also explains that *"the words of a gossip are like choice morsels."* The Hebrew word translated *"choice morsels"* comes from a term meaning "to wound" and can be defined as "to gulp, swallow greedily." These "morsels" may be delicious to the individuals

---

11. "What Does the Bible Say About Gossip?" Got Questions Ministries, https://www.gotquestions.org/gossip-Bible.html.

speaking them, but they are damaging to those being spoken about. They may also be delicious to the hearers who swallow them, but they ultimately wound their inner beings. Although gossip often seems enjoyable at the time, in the end, it causes pain and harm.

> *Those who guard their mouths and their tongues keep themselves from calamity.*   (Proverbs 21:23)

We need to guard our tongues to avoid calamity; therefore, we must be very careful what we choose to say to and about our family members. If our words would be negative or damaging, we should refrain from speaking them, for our own sake as well as other people's. In doing so, we can avoid injured and broken relationships. It is not our job to judge others. That is up to God. Therefore, we do not need to be gossiping about someone else and their private struggles. If that person wants to share any information with others, it is their decision to do so.

ALTHOUGH GOSSIP OFTEN SEEMS ENJOYABLE AT THE TIME, IN THE END, IT CAUSES PAIN AND HARM.

> *A gossip betrays a confidence; so avoid anyone who talks too much.*
>   (Proverbs 20:19)

Scripture warns us to avoid those who habitually gossip because they are betrayers of trust. And remember, it is not easy to rebuild trust in a relationship.

Gossip is denounced not only in the Old Testament but also in the New. For example, in the first chapter of Romans, a list of destructive sins is presented, and gossip is included:

> *Being filled with all unrighteousness, wickedness, greed, evil; full of envy, murder, strife, deceit, malice; they are gossips, slanderers, haters of God, insolent, arrogant, boastful, inventors of evil, disobedient to parents, without understanding, untrustworthy, unloving, unmerciful; and although they know the ordinance of God, that those who practice*

such things are worthy of death, they not only do the same, but also give hearty approval to those who practice them.

(Romans 1:29–32 NASB)

There is no doubt that if we are to refrain from sin and not compound the damaging nature of talebearing, we must avoid both gossip and gossipers. This means we should not stay and listen when someone speaks negatively about another person because then we are partaking in the sin. If it is impossible to leave the conversation, we should try to change the subject as quickly as possible.

But I tell you that everyone will have to give account on the day of judgment for every empty word they have spoken. (Matthew 12:36)

Someday, we will face God in heaven and account for *"every empty word"* we have spoken. Other translations use the term *"careless"* for *"empty."* This means we are going to be accountable for our gossip. If you have engaged in gossip, then repent of your sinful attitudes and behavior and ask God to forgive you. If gossip has become a part of your life, seek God's guidance on how to change your ways. His Holy Spirit can help you learn to guard your tongue.

Without wood a fire goes out; without a gossip a quarrel dies down.

(Proverbs 26:20)

This verse is very applicable to communication in families. Where negative information is shared and there are whisperings of "secrets" about someone, there will often be quarreling. If you want a family that gets along and does not argue, then all gossip needs to cease. When we stop this behavior, other problems will cease as well. In the next chapter, we will explore practical ways to handle negative talk and create a peaceful, uplifting atmosphere in the family.

GOSSIP NEEDN'T BE FALSE TO BE EVIL—THERE'S A LOT OF TRUTH THAT SHOULDN'T BE PASSED AROUND.

—FRANK A. CLARK, U.S. CONGRESSMAN AND LAWYER

CHAPTER RECAP

Scripture tells us, *"A perverse person stirs up conflict, and a gossip separates close friends"* (Proverbs 16:28). Gossip does nothing to foster positive family relationships; it serves only to build walls of hostility and resentment. It violates trust, creates anxiety and tension, produces conflict, distorts the facts, causes division, and compounds problems.

Those who participate in gossip want to share secrets about others for the purpose of producing drama and scandal. Information that is gossiped about is sometimes false and sometimes factual. Either way, it is considered gossip if it damages a person's reputation.

Matthew 12:36 teaches us that we are accountable to God for the words we say, and Proverbs 20:19 counsels, *"A gossip betrays a confidence; so avoid anyone who talks too much."* If we are to refrain from sin and not compound the damaging nature of talebearing, we must avoid both gossip and gossipers. When someone speaks negatively about another person, we should not stay in the conversation because then we are partaking in the sin. If we are unable to leave, we should seek to change the subject as quickly as possible.

QUESTIONS FOR REFLECTION

1. Is gossip a problem in your family? If so, how have your family members reacted to it? What specific negative results have you seen from gossip among family or friends?

2. Have you ever gossiped about a family member? If so, what made you want to do this? After reading this chapter, do you view the situation any differently?

3. What will you do the next time someone begins to gossip about another person in your presence?

7

HOW TO HANDLE NEGATIVE TALK

Not my monkeys, not my circus." This proverb, which indicates, "It is none of my business and I am staying out of it," should become every family's motto. In extended families, there is a tendency to get into one another's business when there is no legitimate reason to. The dynamics of your immediate family, meaning you, your spouse, and your children, are different from those of the immediate families of your siblings or cousins. Each family is distinct. We all have unique ways of parenting and conducting our lives. It is not usually a matter of good or bad, or one way being better than another. It is simply that our ways are different. There is no need to compare, complain, or gossip about the members of our extended family due to our differences. Most gossip is born out of judgment of others. We need to cease judging our family members if we are going to eliminate the destructive behavior of gossip.

My mother is a great example of how to put an end to family gossip. I remember talking to her on the phone one day and mentioning that I had heard through the grapevine something of a personal nature about one of my sisters. When I asked her about it, she said, "It is not my life or news to share. If you want to know, you need to call your sister yourself." My mother ends gossip by guiding people to talk directly to one another. If we have a question about another family member, she will always respond, "Why don't you call them?" She is very kind and matter-of-fact when she says it, but we get the message. Gossip is not a part of her ways and shouldn't be a part of ours either.

If we want to know something about someone, we are to go specifically to that person. It is up to them whether or not they want to share the information with us. In the long run, they will appreciate the fact that we came to them first and didn't gossip through the family. Healthy relationships are those where communications are direct between individuals about issues that concern them.

When you speak directly to someone and hear their perspective, you are less likely to be judgmental and negative about them and more likely to be sensitive to what they are going through. If your desire is to understand them better and not damage the relationship, then one-on-one communication will promote this goal because you will be obtaining information right from the source. When gossip is occurring, there is less of a tendency to seek the point of view of the person who is being talked about. Going straight to the source eliminates gossip altogether.

HEALTHY RELATIONSHIPS ARE THOSE WHERE COMMUNICATIONS ARE DIRECT BETWEEN INDIVIDUALS ABOUT ISSUES THAT CONCERN THEM.

SHUTTING DOWN GOSSIP

When we hear people in our family gossiping, we first need to think about how we will talk with them about this behavior. Will we act judgmental and angry toward them or will we encourage them in a friendly manner to change topics? One good way to shut down gossip is to make those who are spreading it aware of what they are doing and that it should stop. Sometimes, people talk about others out of habit and don't even realize the talk has morphed into inappropriate conversation. You can kindly say to the gossipers, "We probably should not be talking about this person because they would be hurt if they heard what was being said." You can also ask them to put themselves in the shoes of the individual who is the target of the negative talk. "How would you feel if you were the one being talked about like this?"

Remember that whenever someone gossips, you can just excuse yourself from the conversation. They will clearly get the message that you will not participate in negative talk. Gossipers don't like to gossip with those who refuse to join in because it diffuses their drama-creating potential. They want others to eagerly listen and participate in order to make the drama thrive.

If you seek to put an end to family gossip, then you are a drama-killer. That is a good and needed role in all families! Start the trend and help others understand the deep harm that gossip causes.

NOTHING PRODUCTIVE IS EVER ACHIEVED AS A RESULT OF SPREADING, OR LISTENING TO, GOSSIP. DON'T WASTE YOUR TIME! YOU CAN MAKE MORE PRODUCTIVE USE OF IT.
—CATHERINE PULSIFER, "THE PRINCIPLES OF GOSSIP"

WHEN SOMEONE GOSSIPS ABOUT YOU

In the previous chapter, we noted that, in Proverbs, the Bible tells us to avoid the gossiper. However, in Matthew 18, it also tells us that if someone sins against us, we are to go to them to address the problem in hopes of correcting the fault and restoring the relationship. While the immediate context of the following passage is offenses between believers in the church, its general principles can apply to any relationship, and it can be used to address any of the hidden behaviors.

If your brother sins against you, go and tell him his fault, between you and him alone. If he listens to you, you have gained your brother. But if he does not listen, take one or two others along with you, that every charge may be established by the evidence of two or three witnesses. If he refuses to listen to them, tell it to the church. And if he refuses to listen even to the church, let him be to you as a Gentile and a tax

collector. Truly, I say to you, whatever you bind on earth shall be bound
in heaven, and whatever you loose on earth shall be loosed in heaven.

(Matthew 18:15–18 esv)

According to this passage, if someone in the family is gossiping about you, you should address the problem directly with that person. This should be done in private, not in front of a group. Additionally, referring to the person's sin only applies if that individual is also a believer in Christ who recognizes sin and the need to repent from it. If they are not a believer, then you don't address the sin with them in the same manner. They likely won't see it as a sin without the conviction of the Holy Spirit. You might talk with them about it as a damaging behavior. Earlier, we reviewed these biblical guidelines for approaching someone who is involved in wrongdoing:

Brothers, if anyone is caught in any transgression, you who are spiritual
should restore him in a spirit of gentleness. Keep watch on yourself, lest
you too be tempted. Bear one another's burdens, and so fulfill the law of
Christ. (Galatians 6:1–2 esv)

IF SOMEONE IN THE FAMILY IS GOSSIPING ABOUT YOU, YOU SHOULD FIRST ADDRESS THE PROBLEM DIRECTLY AND PRIVATELY WITH THAT PERSON.

If the person persists in gossiping about you, then you need to go to them again, bringing along one or two other family members who have directly heard them or are aware of the gossiping and want it to cease. If the person continues to be unrepentant and refuses to make things right in the relationship and family, then you should take the next step, which is to *"tell it to the church"* (Matthew 18:17). For the original audience of Matthew 18, this meant going to priests or elders. So, if the person is a believer, this step might include going to the pastor or elders of their church if you feel they would be able to help restore the relationship. Such leaders might refer you and your family member to a Christian counselor who is trained in handling family conflict so you can talk through the issue together. If the person isn't a Christian, you might suggest going together to a general family counselor.

If the individual still refuses to change, then you should by all means avoid them. The passage in Matthew 18 talks about treating them as *"a Gentile and a tax collector"* (verse 17). The first-century Jewish hearers of this message did not socialize with these segments of society. So, the passage is saying you can treat the person as though they are not welcome to be a part of your life.

Please understand that I am not saying you should shun the person from your family. However, if a family member is extremely divisive and chooses not to stop their gossiping ways, despite the appeal of other family members, then you should make clear that their gossip is causing damage and undermining the unity of the family, and you need to set up boundaries between them and you. It will be helpful if other family members support a ban of gossip from family gatherings.

Therefore, allow the individual the opportunity to apologize and commit to changing their ways. But if they don't, then they haven't given you many options. God has told us in Proverbs 20:19 to avoid the person who gossips.

We each have to take personal responsibility for family gossip. If we are ones who gossip, we must turn over a new leaf and stop this destructive habit. We need to think before we speak, asking ourselves, "What is the purpose of my message? Is it to spread judgmental or condemning information about others?" If we conclude that there is a negative purpose for the message, then it is gossip and shouldn't be said.

JUDGMENT AND GOSSIP GO HAND IN HAND

I mentioned earlier that when you speak directly to someone about a problem or potential issue rather than gossiping about them, it is less likely that you will be judgmental toward them. This is because judgment and gossip go hand in hand.

Imagine that your brother takes a job in a different state for the summer and unexpectedly becomes engaged to a woman there. He returns home with his fiancée, announcing that they will be married in six short weeks. You don't know anything about this woman and you don't like the fact that your brother is getting married so quickly. You find out her full name and begin to research her history online. Then, you take the information you have gathered to your other siblings so you can discuss your future sister-in-law and what you all think of her.

One of your siblings also does some digging and finds out that this woman may have formerly worked as a dancer at a gentleman's club. Nobody knows if this information is 100 percent true, but it is highly suspected to be the case. The news spreads rapidly through your family. You all now have serious reservations about your brother marrying this woman, especially because he plans to become a pastor.

You decide to take it upon yourself to email him about what you have learned, first and foremost outlining your concerns for him. His reaction is not good. He lashes out at you and says there is no truth to what you are saying and that even if it were true, you are being judgmental and gossiping. After this, the few times that you are with your brother and his fiancée before their wedding are tense. Relationships between your brother, his future wife, and the entire the family are strained.

One problem is that you and your sibling went about digging for dirt on this woman, making assumptions and judging her from the start. What if the information *was* accurate? It still shouldn't have been shared with the entire family. The fiancée's past is her business. You didn't even try to get to know her before you looked for potential problems in her life. In this way, you set up your brother and his future spouse to be defensive from the start. The entire family was wrong to judge this woman and pass around the unflattering information.

This type of scenario occurs in far too many families. One side comes armed with ammunition before relationships can even begin to form. Furthermore, most people have some issue from their past. What right is it of anyone to dig up dirt on others? Especially people you are supposed to be welcoming into the family, not shaming from the get-go.

Another problem is that your brother was confronted via email. When you learned about the fiancée's history and became genuinely concerned, you should have approached your brother personally and privately. A face-to-face meeting would have been best. At the very least, it should have been a phone call. As previously mentioned, words, tone, and motivation can be misinterpreted in an email or text.

A situation like this one can take years to mend. Your interactions with your sister-in-law may thaw over time, but you and the rest of the family are going to have to work to gain her trust and rebuild the relationships with both your brother and his wife.

IF YOU JUDGE PEOPLE,
YOU HAVE NO TIME TO LOVE THEM.
—MOTHER TERESA

JUDGMENT CAN BECOME A PATTERN

When we determine we don't like someone and never will, that individual can never do anything right in our eyes. It becomes easy to find fault in absolutely everything they do in life. Do you feel that way toward a particular family member, where everything they do seems to annoy, irritate, or feel wrong to you? It could be your attitude more than their actions.

Once we make an emotional decision that we are against someone, we hold them to standards that we don't apply to others. We never give them the benefit of the doubt. This kind of attitude creates a wall of contempt within us that prevents us from having a positive relationship with them. If all we ever do is look for the negative in the person and their actions, we will fail to recognize any of their good qualities. And in such a situation, we will be more likely to gossip about them.

When we discover that we have a pattern of judging someone in our family, we need to inspect our heart. Why are we hardening our heart against this individual? What may have caused us to turn against them? What unresolved issues do we have that are causing us to judge everything they do and say?

I have a cousin whom I saw every few months when I was growing up. I wanted to like her, but instead, I would nitpick everything she did and said when we were together. I didn't always speak these criticisms out loud, but the judgments were constantly going on in my mind and heart. I was critical of her clothing, the way she talked, and what she had to say.

After a few years, it dawned on me that I had a hardness in my heart toward her. I started to think about why I was feeling this way. Then I recalled a time when she had made fun of me in front of a group of my other cousins. I remembered feeling mortified and extremely hurt. Although I had pushed the incident out of my mind, it was obviously still affecting my relationship with my cousin years later, manifesting in my negative and judgmental attitudes toward her. I realized that I needed to deal with this issue in my heart. I forgave my cousin for what had happened those many years earlier. Then, I decided I would start looking at her more positively and try to get along with her. Our relationship changed, and she was nicer to me because I was nicer to her. When I decided I would forgive her and work toward fostering a positive connection, it was a vital turning point in our relationship.

BECOME A POSITIVE TALKER AND BUILD OTHERS UP

Another great way to defeat gossip is to employ a principle for creating strong families that applies to all family interactions: talk positively to others and encourage them with uplifting truth. This will help to build relationships and defeat negative talk.

Positive interactions in a family can be contagious. When we seek to lift up a family member, this helps the rest of the family to form positive views of them too. For example, suppose you notice that your sister-in-law is great at baking and always contributes the most delicious desserts to your family gatherings. When she brings her dessert to the next family function, be sure to genuinely compliment her baking skills. You don't have to do it in private either. You can say it in front of other family members. You might be surprised at how far such praise can go toward promoting positive communications in the family. Your brother may then talk about the amazing dessert his wife brought to another family function, offering a second compliment. Gossip breeds negative interactions, while compliments breed positive relationships. Make sure everyone in the family is included in receiving a compliment about something.

The best way to break a negative habit is to replace it with a positive behavior. You can exchange what you might normally say—a disapproving comment or tidbit of gossip—with a positive statement. Thus, to start developing a good relationship with someone whom you don't especially like, begin to look for their good qualities. The next step is to actually affirm those qualities to them. This might not be easy if you have had a difficult relationship with the person, but that is all the more reason to speak positive truths to them, including compliments. Your words and actions of building them up will start to change your relationship for the better. Doing this consistently will encourage positive interactions with all your family members.

> THERE IS NO EXERCISE BETTER FOR THE HEART THAN REACHING DOWN AND LIFTING PEOPLE UP.
> —JOHN F. HOLMES, *IRREGULAR SCOUT TEAM ONE*

For instance, suppose you don't especially like your father-in-law or enjoy being around him. You have complained about him to your sisters-in-law plenty of times in the past. However, you know better now. You understand that such talk only serves to damage relationships in the long run. Therefore, at your next family gathering, you make an effort to avoid negative talk about your father-in-law. Instead, you look for ways you can say something positive directly to him.

You have noticed how he always plays with the grandchildren and gets on their level to communicate and have fun with them, so you tell him, "You are great with all the grandkids. They love being around you and interacting with you." He smiles and thanks you. Then, he goes on to tell you a funny joke. While a positive, thriving relationship between the two of you may not happen overnight, the result of this interaction is an upswing toward a better rapport with your father-in-law. Love and kindness are the answers to divisions in our family relationships, and they are expressed with our words as well as our actions.

TOO OFTEN WE UNDERESTIMATE THE POWER OF A TOUCH, A SMILE, A KIND WORD, A LISTENING EAR, AN HONEST COMPLIMENT, OR THE SMALLEST ACT OF CARING, ALL OF WHICH HAVE THE POTENTIAL TO TURN A LIFE AROUND.

—LEO BUSCAGLIA, *NEW YORK TIMES* BEST-SELLING AUTHOR

CREATE POSITIVE FAMILY EXPERIENCES

An additional method for creating positive family bonds is to build good memories together. If your family members have a difficult time being around one another, then it may be time to adjust your interactions. One thing you can change is your activities. When you get together as a family, perhaps you all sit around the living room of your parents-in-law and talk for hours. Either the conversation seems to turn negative at some point or you are left with a negative feeling afterward. If this is the case, change things up by suggesting fun activities that promote positive interactions and conversations. Choose activities that family members of all ages can participate in and enjoy.

My family has found that volleyball and pool volleyball are sports that almost everyone can participate in. Those who choose to sit on the sidelines can still hang out at the court or pool and cheer along to get in on the fun. Some families like to bowl, hike, golf, swim, roller-skate, sightsee, collect shells on the beach, or play board games. My dad's side of the family always played cards, specifically the game called sheepshead. I have met other families who played different card games on a regular basis. It is a great way to bring people together who have different backgrounds and experiences.

Also, if you have good memories about growing up that you can share, this is a great way to make family get-togethers more positive. Reminiscing about funny, interesting, or heartwarming childhood experiences can lead to an enjoyable time of family bonding. Be sure not to bring up stories that make others look bad. Only bring up memories that make everyone feel uplifted and happy. For example, talking about how your sister took many years to learn how to ride a two-wheel bike and how funny that was to you will not be helpful for enabling everyone to have a pleasant experience together. Your sister may laugh, but inside she may be hurt that you are poking fun at her poor motor skills. To her, it is a flaw in herself that makes her feel bad. Telling a story that makes everyone laugh at the expense of another family member is never a good idea. Focus on stories that are positive and make everyone look good (or at least not bad).

IN TRUTH A FAMILY IS WHAT YOU MAKE IT. IT
IS MADE STRONG, NOT BY NUMBER OF HEADS
COUNTED AT THE DINNER TABLE, BUT BY THE
RITUALS YOU HELP FAMILY MEMBERS CREATE, BY
THE MEMORIES YOU SHARE, BY THE COMMITMENT
OF TIME, CARING, AND LOVE YOU SHOW TO ONE
ANOTHER, AND BY THE HOPES FOR THE FUTURE YOU
HAVE AS INDIVIDUALS AND AS A UNIT.
—MARGE KENNEDY, FAMILIES AND PARENTING AUTHOR

WORDS ARE POWERFUL

Our words matter. They carry weight. They have the power to give life or death to others—not literal life or death, but life or death in terms of feeding a person's innermost being or emotionally killing them.

The tongue has the power of life and death, and those who love it will eat its fruit. (Proverbs 18:21)

The words we speak to our family members can remain with them for a lifetime and influence generations to come. Do we want our words to be loving, comforting, and life-giving, or do we want them to kill the souls of the people whom God gave us to love?

Everyone needs to hear that someone believes in them and their gifts. Family should be a place where people lift you up and always root for you. A person's ability to succeed in life is often based on their ability to persevere. Our perseverance doesn't always come from within. Sometimes, it is the support and encouragement of others that help us to keep going. We need to work on being supportive and encouraging to our family members, believing in their ability to succeed.

Some people feel a need to be the "sounding board of reality" to their family members, presenting only the what ifs instead of also encouraging them and mentioning the positives. For example, imagine you want to publish a children's book. You have wonderful ideas for a story and you are a budding artist. Your parents are very encouraging and believe that you can make it happen. However, your brother asks questions that lean toward the negative, such as "How do you expect to get an agent without any previous publishing experience?" and "Do you think your art skills are good enough for a published children's book?" Even if he brings up some valid points for consideration, the way he expresses them is neither helpful nor uplifting. His response makes you feel that he doesn't support your endeavor. While you know it's important to understand the publishing business and you are in the midst of researching it, you would like him to provide some encouraging words, such as "That is wonderful. If anyone can do it, you can! Let me know if I can help in any way."

Most of us would prefer to hear words of encouragement than statements that question and undermine our abilities, especially when they come from our family members. The world will be our reality check, providing us with enough questions and backlash for any dream we may have. It would be nice to have the guaranteed support of our loved ones. This doesn't mean they should support us in anything illegal or immoral. That is asking too much of any family. However, for our hopes and dreams, our family members should have our back. Everyone needs at least a handful of people who are in their corner cheering them on. If your family does not currently offer this type of support, then perhaps you can be the one to start a positive trend.

Tell your loved ones often that you are proud of them. Your family is not your competition in life. There is an entire world of people who are competing against you, but your family is your team. Even if a family member is serving time in prison, you can find some way to be proud of them. Seriously. People in prison still need to have hope for a future and respect from their families. Look for the positives. At least they are serving their time, taking responsibility, and doing a good job in prison in hopes of being paroled early. They are where they are in life and you are where you are. You don't need to judge, criticize, or compare your life to theirs. The world will tell them how unworthy, unlovable, and awful they are.

Remember, we all need to hear from our family that we are loved and worthy and they are proud of us. When you express pride in the accomplishments of your family members, they find hope. However, never do this falsely. Look for ways that you genuinely believe in them. Often, people who give up on themselves are those who have no one to encourage them. Believing in others will help them believe in themselves.

THERE IS NO GREATER POWER AND SUPPORT YOU CAN GIVE SOMEONE THAN TO LOOK THEM IN THE EYE, AND WITH SINCERITY/CONVICTION SAY, "I BELIEVE IN YOU."
—KEN POIROT, *MENTOR ME*

CHAPTER RECAP

To combat gossip in the family, we need to set a trend of refraining from speaking negative words and innuendo against others. We should also avoid those who perpetually gossip if they refuse to restrain themselves from voicing their negative talk.

A gossip betrays a confidence; so avoid anyone who talks too much.
(Proverbs 20:19)

We can build up our family members by expressing words of support. Look for the good in your loved ones so you can speak uplifting words of truth into their lives. Find ways to create positive family bonds and build good memories together. Our families should be places where we can find encouragement from people who believe in our hopes and dreams. They need to be the primary source where we find consistent positive feedback because the world will provide us with more than enough negativity, disapproval, and discouragement. Believing in our family members will help them believe in themselves.

QUESTIONS FOR REFLECTION

1. Have you fallen into a pattern of criticism or judgment toward a particular family member? Perhaps your dislike of this person has led you to gossip about them. What is the reason for your negative attitude toward them? If you can't think of a specific cause, ask God to show you if there are any unresolved hurts from the past that are contributing to these negative feelings. If so, will you extend forgiveness to this person and give a fresh start to your relationship?

2. What fun activities could your family participate in together to promote more positive interactions and shared memories?

3. Are you supportive of your family members and their abilities, hopes, and dreams? Do you express your support and belief in them? If so, can you provide an example?

HIDDEN BEHAVIOR #4:

DECEPTION

CHAPTER 8

WHEN YOU HAVE VIOLATED SOMEONE'S TRUST

Trust is the rock upon which all relationships exist. If that rock is chipped away among family members by the practice of deception, then over time, the foundation of the family crumbles. However, when a serious form of deception occurs, such as infidelity in a marriage, and that deception is uncovered, the foundation of trust can be broken in an instant. Although it is not easy to rebuild trust and restore a relationship that has been broken by deception, it is possible.

Throughout the Scriptures, we are instructed to conduct our lives with honesty and integrity, and this includes trustworthiness. Here is a sampling of the Bible's wisdom on this topic:

The integrity of the upright guides them, but the unfaithful are destroyed by their duplicity. (Proverbs 11:3)

Do to others as you would have them do to you. (Luke 6:31)

For we are taking pains to do what is right, not only in the eyes of the Lord but also in the eyes of man. (2 Corinthians 8:21)

A TWO-SIDED PROCESS

Whether trust is broken between two friends, a husband and wife, or other family members, both parties must want to work through the brokenness for the relationship to be healed. It is not a one-sided process. If the party who has been wronged does not want to reconcile because the hurt seems too deep, or if the offending party does not want to own up to the wrongdoing that led to the broken trust, the relationship cannot be restored.

Reconciliation requires a great deal from the people involved. Both sides must be willing to come to the table and be open, honest, and vulnerable. They must care enough to put forth the effort needed to make the relationship work again.

If you find yourself in a situation of broken trust, and you and the other party have said yes to restoration, then the following method, which uses the acronym COME FORTH, will help you to become reconciled. You can each become emotionally healthy again, and the relationship may even achieve greater closeness, improved transparency, sincere vulnerability, and open communications to create a better and long-lasting relationship.

THE COME FORTH METHOD

The COME FORTH system works for marriages, other romantic relationships, family relationships, friendships, coworker relationships, and more. The COME component of the method will help the party who is the offender accept responsibility and ask for forgiveness. The FORTH component will help the victim work through the hurt and learn to trust again.

RESTORATION REQUIRES COMMITMENT, VULNERABILITY, OPENNESS, AND A WILLINGNESS TO COMMUNICATE ON THE PART OF BOTH PEOPLE.

In this chapter, we will cover the steps the offender needs to take, and in the next chapter, we will cover the steps the victim needs to take. Again, this is not a quick or easy process. It requires commitment, vulnerability, openness, and a willingness to communicate on the part of both people. When the COME FORTH method is completed correctly, the relationship can be restored.

FOR THE OFFENDER: COME

C: COME CLEAN

Now is the time to come clean about whatever wrong you have done to your loved one, friend, or coworker. If the other person is not yet aware of the wrong, it is best for you to admit your offense and genuinely seek forgiveness before they find out what you did from someone else, which can hurt even more.

> *Whoever walks in integrity walks securely, but whoever takes crooked paths will be found out.* (Proverbs 10:9)

The need for truthfulness and trustworthiness is a common theme in the Bible. The sixth chapter of Proverbs emphasizes seven behaviors that are detestable to God, including not being truthful and breaking trust. In this passage, breaking trust in a relationship could fall under the area of lying, bearing false witness, or stirring up conflict in a community:

> *There are six things the LORD hates, seven that are detestable to him: haughty eyes, a lying tongue, hands that shed innocent blood, a heart that devises wicked schemes, feet that are quick to rush into evil, a false witness who pours out lies and a person who stirs up conflict in the community.* (Proverbs 6:16–20)

ADMIT YOUR WRONGDOING

God calls us to make amends for our wrongs, but He won't force us to do it. You alone can make things right with Him and the individual whose trust you have broken. The first step to coming clean is admitting your transgression to yourself and God. You aren't going to be very good at apologizing to a family member or friend you have wronged if you aren't repentant in your own heart and toward God.

This is a time when you, the offending party, need to do some soul-searching. What was it that caused you to break trust in the relationship? Resist the temptation to blame others. Seek understanding from within yourself. If you look to your inner fears, you are likely to find some answers. For example, if you cheated on your spouse, you may have done so out of fear of abandonment. Your fear of ending up alone may have caused you to seek out another relationship as a backup to your current one. Understanding your fear of abandonment and getting professional help for your own hurt is imperative in the healing process.

Research conducted by the Wharton School, the business school at the University of Pennsylvania, shows that when you admit your wrongdoing, you are more likely to rebuild trust in the relationship after betrayal:

> The experiment found that when a person's trust is violated, and the violation includes deception…it is difficult to restore. "It's okay to screw me over, but don't deceive me as well," says [researcher Eric T.] Bradlow. "If you screw me over and lie about it, it's going to take even longer to recover from it."[12]

WHEN YOU ADMIT YOUR WRONGDOING, YOU ARE MORE LIKELY TO REBUILD TRUST IN THE RELATIONSHIP AFTER BETRAYAL.

If we want reconciliation, then we can't add deception to the equation because deception on top of betrayal makes the situation even worse. This research shows that when we break trust in a relationship, it is much better to own up to the violation than try to cover it up. When deception occurs, then regaining trust becomes much more difficult. That is why we need to confess and admit our wrongdoing rather than continue to deceive the person we have hurt.

---

12. "Promises, Lies and Apologies: Is It Possible to Restore Trust?" Knowledge@Wharton, the Wharton School of the University of Pennsylvania, July 26, 2006, https://knowledge. wharton.upenn.edu/article/promises-lies-and-apologies-is-it-possible-to-restore-trust-2/.

Make sure your heart is in a condition that desires to seek forgiveness and heal the relationship. If you are angry and blame the other person for your wrongdoing in any way, you are likely to cause more division and keep yourself from getting on the right path toward healing and restoration.

KNOW WHAT YOU'RE GOING TO SAY

Before you approach the individual to come clean, know what you are going to say. Pray to God and seek His wisdom. Ask Him to guide your heart and speech. To gain insights on what God would say concerning the situation, ask your pastor and go to the Bible. You can conduct an online search for Bible concordances and commentaries that can help you learn about the subject you are dealing with and what the Scriptures have to say about it.

For example, if you have broken trust by lying about someone, read some applicable Scripture passages. Then, ask God for forgiveness, commit the issue to Him, and rely on Him to help you restore your relationship with the person whom you have hurt. He will help you find the words and strength to have the difficult conversation.

Years ago, I sent an unkind text message to a family member. I was hurt by something she had done to me and I reacted badly. You can imagine how much that helped the situation. It didn't! For the next few days, God convicted me about that text message. My response to Him was, "Well, it was sent, so I can't unsend it now."

Yet God clearly told me I needed to apologize…and not merely text an apology. I had to call my family member and express my sincere regret and desire to work toward mending the relationship. It was not easy, especially because I felt she had committed the first wrong and should be apologizing to me. However, as I have noted, we cannot control the actions of others. We only have control over our own behavior. Therefore, I knew I had to do the right thing in the situation and call her.

Before I dialed the number, I went to God in prayer and asked Him to soften my heart toward my family member regarding this situation. I also asked Him to give me the words that needed to be said to restore the relationship. He gave me those words, which I jotted down on a piece of paper.

A peace came over me, and I sensed that making this call was exactly what I needed to be doing.

When I called my family member and apologized, to my surprise, she apologized as well. I did not expect that to happen. However, because I took the first step in contacting her and saying I was sorry, it made her feel open and trusting to express her own remorse to me. It helped our relationship and we turned the corner on developing a friendship.

AFFIRM THE OTHER PERSON'S VALUE

When you talk with the person, be sure to start out by letting them know how much you value your relationship with them, which is why you are confessing. Talk about your past together, the importance of the relationship for both of you, and the need to get through this situation to have a fresh start together. If you preface your talk with this perspective, it should help to put the other person in a better frame of mind for accepting the information and also demonstrate your willingness to heal the relationship. Simply blurting out something like "I cheated on you" will probably lead to an argument that might include yelling and screaming. So again, start the conversation by talking about your genuine love, affection, or care for the individual.

BE SENSITIVE TO THE SITUATION

Additionally, be willing to acknowledge your wrongdoing in a sensitive manner. For example, if the violation you are coming clean about is infidelity, then you should admit your unfaithfulness without giving graphic details. Your spouse does not need to know specific information about liaisons and sexual encounters.

Understand that once you provide those details, they cannot be erased from your loved one's mind and they may leave a lasting scar on their soul, doing further harm rather than bringing healing. This additional hurt will make it harder for them to overcome the betrayal. Instead, come clean about the basics and keep the focus of the conversation on your desire to change and your commitment to never offend in this manner again. Adopt a personal zero-tolerance policy toward deception, deceit, and infidelity in the future. However, do answer all of the other person's questions, responding openly and honestly. Your goal is to show you are willing to be 100 percent transparent for the sake of the relationship moving forward.

If the person you are confessing your trust violation to has been violent in the past or you fear a physical or violent reaction, make sure not to talk to them alone, putting yourself in harm's way. Use your best judgment, considering your safety and life to be of utmost importance.

COME CLEAN ABOUT THE BASICS AND KEEP THE FOCUS OF THE CONVERSATION ON YOUR DESIRE TO CHANGE AND YOUR COMMITMENT TO NEVER OFFEND IN THIS MANNER AGAIN.

DON'T WITHHOLD THE TRUTH

As we discussed earlier, withholding the truth about a transgression can be even more detrimental to a relationship than the actual violation. Be sure to keep this fact in mind because not admitting to your wrongdoing may prevent your relationship from ever being restored. Know your priorities. Do you want a good relationship? Do you want the hurts to be healed? If the answer is yes, then coming clean and admitting your offense is foundational to the process.

A couple whom I will call Scott and Jane couldn't even begin the COME FORTH method for healing their marriage because Scott failed to admit to his infidelity. Jane had undeniable proof of his multiple affairs over the years, including his current affair, in which he was seeing a woman from his previous place of work. This woman had moved to another state, and Scott had been communicating with her for months through private messages on social media. In those messages, which Jane found on their home computer, meet-up times and dates of the affair were discussed. It was clear that Scott had been traveling on "work trips" to see this other woman and that he not only had an emotional relationship with her but also a sexual one. Even after being confronted with this proof, Scott would not admit to the affair. He claimed that the communications were "all talk, and nothing physical ever happened."

Scott always made excuses regarding the evidence of his affairs, and Jane was tired of his blatant lies. She was willing to work through the crisis if he would admit to his wrongdoing and seek help, including marriage counseling, but he still refused to own up to anything. This couple stayed together for a few more years, but those years were miserable, as both would admit. There was no resolution to the infidelity. It was like a black cloud that continually loomed over their relationship. Eventually, Scott left Jane for another woman with whom he was having an affair, and the couple divorced. Even then, Scott never did acknowledge his cheating.

Apparently, Scott didn't admit to his unfaithfulness because he never had any intention of changing his ways. Even when Jane became more confrontational about the evidence of his cheating, it didn't alter his behavior. If anything, it just made him more secretive about his affairs. The couple's relationship had the potential to be healed because Jane was willing to forgive and work with Scott if he would acknowledge his wrongdoing and stop the cheating. She was hopeful, but in the end, they were divorced because Scott had no desire to come clean, discontinue his affairs, and renew his relationship with Jane.

SHOW GENUINE REMORSE

When you confess your wrongdoing, you also need to demonstrate genuine remorse by being apologetic and sincerely penitent. If you aren't feeling remorseful, then you need to take an honest assessment of your actions and how they have affected others. Try to put yourself in the shoes of the person you have hurt. How would you feel if the situation were flipped and you were the one whose trust had been broken?

Find the courage to demonstrate your contrition through a sincere, thoughtfully worded apology. Explain that you regret your actions and have determined never to repeat them. Mean what you say by doing what you say. Trust cannot be regained unless your actions match your words.

For example, imagine that you fail to include your sister-in-law in a ladies-only spa day with your two sisters and mother. Your reason for not including her is that she is married into the family, so your relationship with her is different from those with your sisters and mom. However, your brother calls after the fact to let you know that not including your sister-in-law has seriously hurt her feelings. He says that his wife feels like a less-than-equal member of the family when she is excluded from such gatherings. Her sense of trust that she is accepted by her in-laws has been fractured.

Your brother's wife is the only sister-in-law in the family, and you didn't realize it would bother her not to be invited. However, now that you know she is hurt, you want to restore the relationship. When you call her to apologize, you don't make excuses by saying you thought she wouldn't want to spend her Saturday with her in-laws or that she never expressed an interest in going on a spa day before. Instead, you own up to your wrongdoing. You avoid excuses and blaming her in any way, saying, "I am so sorry we didn't include you; we will make sure you are included in all future gatherings because you are family and we love you." The sincerity of your tone is what will help to restore the relationship, along with the fulfillment of the promise to always include her moving forward.

Therefore, you cannot merely state what you have done wrong and make excuses for the behavior or, worse yet, blame the victim. You must take responsibility for your actions, admit your wrongdoing, and ask for forgiveness in a genuine manner.

TRUST CANNOT BE REGAINED UNLESS YOUR ACTIONS MATCH YOUR WORDS.

EXPECT A PAINFUL REACTION

When you come clean, expect a painful reaction from the other person. Prepare yourself for the emotions and words that may be expressed. The level of reaction you receive will likely correlate with the level of hurt you have inflicted. There may be tears, sobbing, harsh words, and even yelling. No matter what the reaction, do not respond with anything other than empathy and care. You don't want to make things worse by becoming heated and reacting with negative words or actions. Remain composed and keep a level head. Know that the other person's emotions will eventually quiet down.

Be the calming force in the storm. You want the relationship to work, so you need to be strong when you experience the other person's reaction. You can reaffirm how sorry you are and how much you care for the person, which is why you have come clean and want to make things right in the relationship.

One research study identified empathy, humility, commitment, and apology as four core elements needed for healing a marriage after infidelity occurs. These four elements must be exemplified especially by the person who committed the adultery.[13] Adultery is just one example of broken trust that requires these elements for restoration. In any relationship, if these features are genuinely demonstrated by the person who violated the trust to the person whom they have hurt or wronged, it will help to heal the hurt and release bitterness and anger.

For example, if you want to apologize to your father because you said insulting things to him regarding his new wife, then you don't begin by saying something like, "I'm sorry, but it's true. She did date a lot of men before you!" Don't add insult to injury if you sincerely want the relationship to be restored. Your father is likely to respond with anger if your apology includes more insults or blame. Instead, say, "I'm sorry I said those things to you about your wife. It was insulting, unkind, and wrong of me. I won't do it again."

Remember, the tone of your voice is important, so sincerity in the delivery of your message is crucial. Humility will come across in your tone if you are truly humble. Similar to the illustration about the brother whose family gossiped about his fiancé's past, if you desire to have a good relationship with your father and his new wife, you must realize that bringing up negative aspects of your stepmother's life is not helpful. When you genuinely apologize and determine never to bring up the subject again, you will help to restore and strengthen those relationships.

O: OPEN YOURSELF EMOTIONALLY

Once you have completed the first step of coming clean about your offense, the next step is to be open emotionally. Ask for forgiveness and

---

13. Stephen T. Fife, Gerald R. Weeks, and Jessica Stellberg-Filbert, "Facilitating Forgiveness in the Treatment of Infidelity: An Interpersonal Model," *Journal of Family Therapy*, 35, no. 4, 343–67.

then listen to the thoughts and emotions of the person whom you have hurt.

Listen with empathy. Once more, avoid any knee-jerk reactions to defend yourself. The offended party needs to get these words off their chest to process their hurt. Hear with a heart that is willing to see what you did wrong, a desire to never hurt them in this manner again, and a willingness to help them process their hurt by simply listening with understanding.

Asking for forgiveness may not be a onetime event—especially when the other person is talking about how you have hurt them. The necessity for more apologizing will correspond to the level of hurt you have inflicted. What you are apologizing for are the various ways you have caused the hurt.

For example, in a case of infidelity, your spouse may now realize that you weren't missing family dinners because you had to attend evening business meetings but because you were having an affair. The truth of the infidelity and affair is one hurt; lying about skipping meals is another. Furthermore, the hurt is compounded because you considered this other person with whom you cheated to be more important than your own family. Apologizing for each wrong and listening with empathy will help the healing process to begin.

M: MAKE MEANINGFUL CONVERSATIONS

When the other party's emotions have calmed down and their anger has begun to subside, they may be willing to hear why you did what you did. Again, as you talk to the victim about your offense, it is never appropriate to place blame on them. Instead, use what was revealed to you in your soul-searching process as a starting point for meaningful talks. If the other person cares for you and your relationship, then they will want to help you process whatever fears or emotional difficulties you are experiencing that caused you to violate their trust.

Talk openly about those fears. To build on a previous example, if the reason you cheated on your spouse wasn't that you didn't find them appealing anymore but because you have a fear of abandonment, express those feelings. The other person deserves to understand why the situation happened. Talking with you will help ease the burden of responsibility from them. It will enable them to realize they were not the issue. If they never learn why you committed the betrayal, they may harbor feelings of self-blame. Explain your side of the situation so they can put themselves in your shoes, but remember to do so with humility, candor, and empathy toward them.

For another illustration of a hidden root issue that can lead to conflict, let's look at the case of Brock and Emily (not their real names). Emily had been married previously. Her marriage had ended because of repeated infidelity by her husband. Now that she and Brock had been married for five years, they were running into some bumps in the road. The issues were mostly minor, such as parenting differences that could easily be resolved. However, the conflict kept escalating and Emily began threatening divorce in every argument. This became a weekly occurrence, so the couple began counseling.

At first, Emily did not even understand why she was threatening to get a divorce because she didn't actually *want* a divorce. In counseling, she came to realize that she was reacting this way because she didn't feel heard by Brock. He would brush off her parenting concerns or dismiss them entirely. In her previous marriage, whenever problems arose, Emily's ex-husband had threatened her with divorce. She recalled how each time he made that threat, it had made her desperate to change whatever he claimed she was doing to cause problems in their marriage, whether it was spending too much time with friends or traveling too frequently for work, because the idea of divorce scared her. It turned out that she was very angry at Brock for not taking her parenting concerns seriously. She took a very harsh approach to get his attention, much like Emily's previous husband had done to her. However, threatening divorce *had* made Brock take her seriously, and it had also landed them in counseling.

As a result, Brock began to discuss Emily's parenting concerns with her rather than brushing them off. In counseling, they also discovered together that Emily's reaction of threatening divorce stemmed from learned behavior in her previous marriage. Emily realized this tactic was highly damaging to her relationship with her husband and she needed to discontinue using it. The counseling sessions enabled her to understand why she was doing what she was doing and also helped the couple develop more open lines of communication for dealing with their problems. It was Emily's fear of not being heard about issues she deemed of high importance that had led to her threats of divorce. When Brock and Emily developed better communication and understood where Emily's fear stemmed from, their marriage improved.

From this scenario, we see again how understanding the root cause of a violation of trust can help those who have been victimized feel less burdened by any feelings of responsibility for it. The goal is to recognize the underlying emotional or psychological issues at work so that healing can happen.

EXPLAIN YOUR SIDE OF THE SITUATION SO THE OTHER PERSON CAN PUT THEMSELVES IN YOUR SHOES, BUT REMEMBER TO DO SO WITH HUMILITY, CANDOR, AND EMPATHY TOWARD THEM.

E: ENGAGE IN FULL TRANSPARENCY OF YOUR LIFE

The fourth obligation for the person who has broken trust in a relationship is to provide full transparency of their life. If you are the offending party and want the other person to trust you again, then decide that you will be completely open, even before asking for forgiveness.

Transparency can go a long way toward restoring trust. For example, if you are part of a charity planning event and temporarily took money from the event for personal use because you were short on cash, then you need to be fully transparent about the accounts and paperwork with the other individuals working on the event so that everyone involved knows that trust can be regained. If you aren't hiding anything, then this should not be a problem. The same transparency will be needed moving forward if you retain your position in the charity.

If the trust violation involves infidelity, then you should provide full transparency regarding your phone records, texts, social media accounts, and email accounts. This means you freely give your spouse your passwords and allow them access to your phone and any other mode of Internet use, whether it is a computer, laptop, or tablet, so they can check on things whenever they choose. Your willingness to be transparent and provide any information that was previously unknown or hidden to them will help them regain trust.

If you are unwilling to be transparent, then you need to do some self-examination. Are you seeking to hide something? What don't you want the other party to know? Withholding another wrong you have committed will make transparency very difficult. If you need to confess to something else, there is no better time than the present to do it. Full transparency means that you have admitted to everything and there is nothing further to uncover because you are willingly giving the other party access to your life in real time.

The study I referenced earlier in this chapter from the Wharton School at the University of Pennsylvania also found that in a situation of broken trust, when meaningful change is exemplified by the transgressor, the victim is more likely to begin trusting again:

> Trust harmed by untrustworthy behavior can be effectively restored when individuals observe a consistent series of trustworthy actions, the researchers conclude. Also, making a promise to change behavior can help speed up the trust recovery process.[14]

This research shows that making promises to change while also demonstrating an effort to change will help bring healing. Thus, trust can be steadily regained when the changes in behavior are both meaningful and dependable.

IT IS THE NEGLECT OF TIMELY REPAIR THAT MAKES REBUILDING NECESSARY.
—RICHARD WHATELY, ENGLISH THEOLOGIAN, EDUCATOR, RHETORICIAN, AND SOCIAL REFORMER

----

14. "Promises, Lies and Apologies," Knowledge@Wharton.

CHAPTER RECAP

Trust is the foundation of relationships, especially in the family. That is why, when trust is broken, lives can be broken. However, if there has been a violation of trust, there is still hope. Restoration can happen if the right steps are taken. The COME FORTH method provides steps for both the offender and the victim to take actions toward healing the relationship. Healing can occur even in the most broken situations when God is invited into the process.

For the offender, the process is "COME": (1) come clean, (2) open yourself emotionally, (3) make meaningful conversations, and (4) engage in full transparency.

QUESTIONS FOR REFLECTION

1. If you have violated someone's trust, have you made an effort to be honest and restore the relationship? If so, what was the result? Why do you think this was the result?

2. If you have broken trust with someone but have done little or nothing about it, how can you take the first steps toward restoring the relationship based on the COME FORTH method?

3. What do you personally find most helpful about the "COME" portion of the COME FORTH method? Why?

CHAPTER 9

HOW TO RECOVER FROM BROKEN TRUST

In this chapter, we continue the COME FORTH method from the perspective of the victim of the deception. This method applies to all types of broken trust, from misunderstandings between friends to adultery in a marriage. As I mentioned in chapter 8, reconciliation after broken trust takes commitment on both sides. Before you begin the process of restoring the relationship, ask yourself, "Is this person and the relationship I had with them worth the emotional effort?" Only you can answer this question.

However, please keep in mind that God has said we should make every effort to have peace among all people.

If it is possible, as far as it depends on you, live at peace with every-one. (Romans 12:18)

Make every effort to live in peace with everyone and to be holy; without holiness no one will see the Lord. (Hebrews 12:14)

It is important to seek peace in relationships where trust has been broken. Again, this means reconciling the relationships if possible. This does not mean that someone who betrays you is instantly given back 100 percent of your trust after they apologize. Instead, it means you forgive them for their wrongs and set new boundaries. Your relationship has a new start, but in a changed way. You can't force the other person to make peace with you, but you can do your part to heal the relationship by forgiving.

Research from Northwestern University has shown that people who are more trusting by nature are more likely to be forgiving and forgetful of others' failures.

> People who are highly trusting tended to remember transgressions in a way that benefits the relationship, remembering partner transgressions as less severe than they originally reported them to be. People low on trust demonstrated the opposite pattern, remembering partner transgressions as being more severe than how they originally reported them to be.[15]

This research gives hope to relationships where trust has been violated. Rebuilding trust with the offender in an open and honest way is imperative for the victim because it will help shape the way they view the betrayal in the future. The effects may be less damaging and long-lasting.

FOR THE VICTIM: FORTH

F: FORGIVE

For the victim, forgiveness is the first step in healing a relationship. We discussed the benefits of forgiveness in depth in chapter 2, so I encourage you to review that chapter after reading this section. Holding on to hate, anger, and other negative feelings will only make you feel worse. Release those feelings by allowing yourself to forgive. This doesn't mean that there won't be consequences for the offending party for the violation of your trust, especially in more serious situations. You will come to an agreement about those consequences while engaging in meaningful conversations with the other person. For example, as described in the previous chapter, in a situation where infidelity has occurred, you can ask the person to be transparent about their phone, email, and other Internet use moving forward.

Remember that God tells us to forgive others:

---

15. Hilary Hurd Anyaso, "Trust Makes You Delusional, and That's Not All Bad," *Northwestern Now*, February 27, 2013, https://news.northwestern.edu/stories/2013/02/trust-makes-you-delusional-and-thats-not-all-bad.

Bear with each other and forgive one another if any of you has a griev-
ance against someone. Forgive as the Lord forgave you.

(Colossians 3:13)

For if you forgive other people when they sin against you, your heavenly
Father will also forgive you. But if you do not forgive others their sins,
your Father will not forgive your sins.   (Matthew 6:14–15)

God tells us to forgive others for our own good. If we lack forgiveness
and hold on to ill will against someone, we keep a wall between ourselves
and God. He wants us to be close to Him, so we need to extend forgiveness
to the one who has wronged us. Again, this doesn't mean we won't establish
boundaries with them because of their actions, but it does mean we won't
harbor bitterness or resentment. We need to let go of the wrong that has
occurred and not hold grudges. God says He will not forgive our sins if we
do not forgive those who have sinned against us.

Get rid of all bitterness, rage and anger, brawling and slander, along
with every form of malice. Be kind and compassionate to one another,
forgiving each other, just as in Christ God forgave you.

(Ephesians 4:31–32)

HOLDING ON TO HATE, ANGER, AND OTHER NEGATIVE FEELINGS WILL ONLY MAKE YOU FEEL WORSE.

It can be very difficult to forgive. For severe transgressions, such as infidelity or abuse, it will mean a constant process of turning over your hurt to
God and asking Him to help you move forward without retaining any hard
feelings. It may take months or even years to heal your heart. However,
know that you are doing as God has asked by forgiving and asking for His
help in your healing process. You don't have to do this alone. He can provide the comfort and strength you need if you will ask Him and keep giving
your feelings over to Him as often as needed. Every time hurt or bitterness

resurfaces, ask God to release it and soften your heart toward the one who has sinned against you. Take note that in situations involving any type of abuse, you will also need counseling in order to achieve healing.

Forgiveness also means that you care enough for the person who broke your trust that you want to work with them emotionally to process the pain and restore the relationship (whenever possible). If you aren't willing to forgive, then the relationship is forever changed and likely will never be what it once was. A true, healthy restoration cannot occur unless forgiveness is present.

Just as unforgiveness creates a wall between us and God, it creates a barrier between us and the offender. In forgiveness, you need to be willing to take down that barrier. The relationship will only improve if you have taken the step to forgive. Doing so demonstrates to the other person how much you value them. The bigger the offense, the harder it will be, but forgiveness may also make the relationship that much deeper.

What should you do if the offender hasn't acknowledged their wrongdoing? It is often the case that the transgression is revealed before the person who broke the trust admits to what they have done. You should still give them the chance to come clean and make things right. This means you must be willing to forgive even before they admit their wrongdoing. However, the process of reconciliation still hinges on the other person's willingness to admit their wrong when it is brought to light.

DISCUSS THE MATTER WITH THE PERSON

Thus, if someone has broken your trust and you find out about it, you need to go to that person to discuss the matter. How you present the issue is of great importance. If you approach them with self-righteous anger, then the outcome of the conversation is not likely to result in an admission of their wrongs, nor will it help to start the healing process.

Before you talk to the person, refer again to the model for reconciliation that Jesus gave us in Matthew 18. The first stage is found in verse 15:

> If your brother sins against you, go and tell him his fault, between you and him alone. If he listens to you, you have gained your brother.
>
> (Matthew 18:15 ESV)

We are instructed to speak to the individual one-on-one. Do not involve anyone else, especially not a large group of people. If you take someone with you, the offending party will probably feel you are ganging up on them. They will be more likely to react defensively and close themselves off emotionally to protect themselves. Of course, the exception to this principle is a situation where the person has exhibited violence in the past or might become violent. Then, you need to bring someone else for your own safety. In this case, utilize the help of professionals. As I recommended in an earlier chapter, you can contact the National Resource Center on Domestic Violence at https://nrcdv.org.

Talk with the person who has broken trust in a manner that lets them know you want them to acknowledge their wrongdoing so your relationship can be restored. (This is the equivalent of the "Come Clean" step for the offender in the first part of the COME FORTH method.) Think of it as a heart-to-heart talk. Remember to approach them with empathy. You never know what types of issues they are dealing with in their heart and mind. Give them the courtesy of kind words and a calm tone of voice. If you value the relationship, then you will place great importance on this conversation because it has the potential to destroy the relationship altogether or contribute to healing and a stronger bond.

THE OFFENDER MIGHT NEED A FEW DAYS TO A FEW WEEKS TO ACKNOWLEDGE THEIR WRONGDOING AND APOLOGIZE, DEPENDING ON THE SITUATION AND SEVERITY OF THE OFFENSE.

If the individual does not readily admit their transgression or apologize, give them some time. This might be a few days to a few weeks depending on the situation and severity of the offense. As we discussed earlier, people do not always admit their wrongdoing immediately. They may need time to consider their actions and may acknowledge their transgression only after an initial discussion of the matter. You can let them know you understand this dynamic as you conclude your conversation, saying, "I can see you are not ready to admit to breaking my trust at this time, but I will give you a few days to think things over and get back to me because I value our relationship and want to restore the broken trust together." Giving the person grace and mercy is the right thing to do if you care for them and the relationship.

TAKE ONE OR TWO OTHERS

If, after a period of allowing them to digest your conversation, the person still refuses to admit to their wrongdoing, then you can approach them again with one or two others. This is the wise guidance of Scripture:

> *But if he does not listen, take one or two others along with you, that every charge may be established by the evidence of two or three witnesses.* (Matthew 18:16 ESV)

If you need to bring in others to help with mediation after you have already spoken with the offender, make sure you bring those who are appropriate to the circumstance. Matthew 18:16 explains that we should take people who are potential witnesses to the situation. If the person you bring along is a friend who has nothing directly to do with the problem, this might not be helpful.

Therefore, keep the restoration of your relationship foremost in mind when you ask another person to go with you. Take a fellow family member who is a witness to the situation and also likely to be able to help with reconciliation. Do not take someone who is likely to meddle or stir things up further between you and the individual who has broken trust. Again, this action of bringing along another person is only to be taken after you have approached the offender privately and they have been unresponsive.

APPEAL TO AN AUTHORITY

If the person continues to deny any wrongdoing or you feel the relationship has not been mended, you can take it to the next level.

> *If he refuses to listen to them, tell it to the church. And if he refuses to listen even to the church, let him be to you as a Gentile and a tax collector.* (Matthew 18:17)

This stage involves seeking someone of higher authority for counsel. For example, in the case of infidelity, you could arrange to see a marriage counselor. If it is an offense by a coworker, you could ask a supervisor or boss to mediate the situation. If it is a breach in a friendship and the two of you attend the same church, you could seek counsel from your pastor, an elder, or another mature believer who might be willing to mediate a discussion. Again, the goal is to help the person see that you care about them and the relationship and want them to deal with the violation of trust so the relationship can continue.

Let's look at the case of Rick and Mary (not their real names). Mary had been cheating on Rick with a man from her workplace. Rick found out about the cheating and confronted Mary, but she denied the allegation. Rick did the right thing and waited. He had sought counsel from his pastor, who told him not to take any action immediately following his discussion with Mary. The pastor had experience and told him that, for many people, time is needed when it comes to making the decision to admit their infidelity. Rick had faith that his wife would acknowledge what she had done and reconcile the relationship if given the time and opportunity.

Mary did some soul-searching and also sought my advice. My response was that she needed to return to her husband, not only for the sake of her marriage but also for her children. However, I didn't tell her all that outright. Instead, I helped her look at her situation objectively and consider all the people involved. Mary needed to assess the reality of the situation and the character of the individual with whom she was involved. She also needed time to come to her own conclusion that restoring her marriage was the best decision. Mary came clean to Rick a few days after he confronted her.

Not all spouses are as understanding as Rick was. However, knowing that Rick wanted to heal the marriage helped Mary repent and return to her marriage and family. For the past few months, she had been present in the home physically, but she had checked out of the marriage emotionally and had been planning to leave her husband. Rick's steadfastness in wanting to heal the marriage if she would admit her wrongs and work through their problems in marriage counseling was an important factor in the process of Mary's decision-making. It helped greatly that Rick had not given her an ultimatum on the day he confronted her. If he had, their marriage might well have ended in divorce. Instead, he gave her the time she needed to consider her options and confront the reality of where her decisions would lead.

Rick and Mary are still married, and they are doing better than ever. People make mistakes. It is the reaction to those mistakes by both parties involved that affects the eventual outcome. If the party who has been hurt has a severe reaction to the deception, then there may be little hope for healing. Again, if Rick had given Mary an ultimatum and made her choose on the spot between him and the other man, Mary wouldn't have had time to process everything and make the right choice. Although she initially denied the affair, she eventually admitted it in order to heal her marriage. Even though Rick might have been justified in issuing an ultimatum, it would not have served their marriage well. His wisdom in allowing Mary to reflect provided her the opportunity to seek advice and counsel from others, including me. But she herself made the final decision to stay in her marriage.

What if the person who broke trust is still unwilling to come clean after you have gone through all these stages of reconciliation? Many marriages have continued for years in spite of trust violations such as infidelity, without the cheater admitting their wrongdoing. However, the relationship is never the same. There will always be a lack of true intimacy. As mentioned in the previous chapter, sometimes the offending party's failure to admit their wrongdoing can be even more harmful than the violation that initially broke the trust.

PEOPLE MAKE MISTAKES. IT IS THE REACTION TO THOSE MISTAKES BY THE PARTIES INVOLVED THAT AFFECTS THE EVENTUAL OUTCOME.

You can maintain forgiveness in your heart toward the person who offended you even if you do not receive an admission of wrongdoing or an apology. This will enable you to experience healing from your pain and move forward in life without harboring any resentment. The individual's lack of apology or refusal to acknowledge their guilt will result in a broken relationship, or one that is very damaged, depending on the depth of the wrongdoing and level of deception. However, you are doing yourself a favor when you forgive. You are unburdening any feelings of ill will or hurt that resulted from this person violating your trust. You are also choosing not to hold on to anger, bitterness, and resentment.

O: OPEN CONVERSATIONS

If the other person admits to their wrongdoing, the second step is to share with them the ways in which they have hurt you. A word to the wise: do not begin the blame game. It is best to express yourself with statements that start with "I feel" rather than "You did this" or "You said that." In this way, you will be approaching the individual with your personal emotions rather than attacking them about what they have done. If the other person feels accused, they will probably go on the defensive, and productive healing will be unlikely to occur during the conversation. Pointing fingers will not be helpful in the overall process of restoring trust.

Therefore, before you speak to the person about the offense, take time to process what you are thinking and feeling. Then, decide on which words and phrases you will use. Write down specific "I feel" statements. Make sure that what you say is spoken with the intention of restoration, not alienation. Use a calm tone of voice and the "I feel" statements you have prepared to convey your feelings of hurt about the actions that violated your trust.

Suppose you are dealing with a close friend who threw a party to which you were not invited. You can begin by saying, "I saw the photos of your party on social media and I feel hurt that I wasn't invited." You can then follow up with a question that will open the conversation to a deeper level: "Is there something I did to hurt you or our relationship that was perhaps the reason I wasn't invited?" Allow the other person to respond. If they care about you and your friendship, they will want to explain and apologize if necessary.

There could be a simple explanation. For example, the party might only have been for friends from the person's college years. You won't know the answer unless you ask. However, do so with kindness, grace, and understanding so that you can have a better relationship moving forward.

Make sure you ask all the questions you want to from the person who violated your trust and receive answers. Having unanswered questions can prevent you from healing. If you and the other person are working together to restore the relationship, they should be willing to answer your questions.

As expressed in chapter 8, with infidelity, you don't need to know specifics of an intimate nature; that would not be helpful. However, you may be wondering where and how the affair began. You want to know this information so you won't imagine that it might have been at the gym and become concerned every time your spouse leaves the house to do a workout.

Having this type of question answered can give you peace of mind, especially if you can fortify the relationship with expectations of transparency moving forward. If you find out the affair did begin at the gym, then one solution might be for your spouse to change gyms so they won't run into the person with whom they committed adultery. Perhaps you and your spouse could commit to going to a gym together to work out. That might give you a new way to spend more time with one another and also solve your problem of being afraid your spouse might meet someone else every time they go to the gym.

R: REQUEST WHAT YOU NEED TO GET BACK TO A HEALTHY RELATIONSHIP

This step goes hand in hand with having open conversations with the offender. You should discuss not only what happened but also how things can be resolved. This means talking about why the trust was broken, what is required to heal the relationship, and how it will work moving forward.

It is important that your requirements and expectations for the other party be reasonable. If you raise the bar too high, you are setting the person and relationship up for failure. For example, if your spouse was unfaithful, you can't expect them never talk to someone of the opposite sex ever again. Setting that rule or expectation would be unreasonable. It would also likely be broken the first day, which means you will feel further violated and the trust will have been undermined once more.

Therefore, discuss these matters without making demands. Instead, talk about what would make you feel comfortable and would help to rebuild trust. If the other party cares enough, they will be willing to meet reasonable requests.

IT IS IMPORTANT THAT YOUR REQUIREMENTS AND EXPECTATIONS FOR THE OTHER PARTY BE REASONABLE. IF YOU RAISE THE BAR TOO HIGH, YOU ARE SETTING THE PERSON AND RELATIONSHIP UP FOR FAILURE.

A couple I will name Al and Karen provide a good example of making an unreasonable request. They had been married only a few months when Al's mom came over to help Karen finish unpacking and organize their new home while Al was at work. Karen and her mother-in-law had previously gotten along just fine. However, their relationship took a negative turn that day when Al's mother made critical comments to Karen about her taste and style of decorating. Karen was deeply hurt. After her mother-in-law left, she told Al that if their marriage was going to work, his mother was never to be allowed in their home again. Ever. If Al didn't agree to this, she would divorce him. Divorce wasn't an option for him, so he reluctantly agreed.

This arrangement lasted about six months. Eventually, Karen realized the ban was actually stressing her marriage, especially since the couple lived in the same town as Al's parents. Her mandate of never allowing the in-laws in her home was both unreasonable and unrealistic, and it was hurting her relationship with her husband. Al resented the fact that she had made such a severe request, but he didn't know how to change her mind. It was a situation that was making Al have to choose between his wife and his mother.

Marriage counseling helped this couple. After a few sessions together, they invited Al's parents into a session. During that meeting, realistic boundaries were set for Karen's mother-in-law. These limitations were mainly about giving advice and criticizing. She was invited back into Al and Karen's home, but a hard line was drawn in the sand. If Al's mom went back to criticizing, she would not be welcome there.

The relationship between Karen and her in-laws improved over time. It took years to develop a deeper relationship of trust. But this trust developed because Al's mother abided by her word for the most part and did not criticize or give unsolicited advice to Karen.

T: TALK ABOUT THE BETRAYAL TO A CONFIDANT OR PROFESSIONAL

When your trust has been broken, you should also seek wise counsel on the matter. Talking with someone else will help you gain a better understanding of the situation and your own feelings. It will also help you process your emotions. Allow yourself to open up to someone who can assist you through these circumstances. Speaking with a professional such as a counselor or pastor is always a wise choice when seeking help about deeply personal matters.

In the earlier example of Rick and Mary, both parties sought help and counsel from others. Because Rick went to his pastor for guidance, he didn't make the mistake of giving Mary an ultimatum or doing anything irrational, and this helped to save his marriage. When the issue is severe, such as infidelity or abuse, counseling for both parties is highly recommended.

Don't keep your feelings inside. Broken trust can bring up all sorts of emotions and even unresolved issues from the past. When you never unburden yourself by talking through your feelings, you allow those emotions to fester. If you are unwilling to open up, the wound may become even more painful. Go to someone whom you trust and talk to them about what has happened. Commit to working through your emotions so you can move on.

H: HEAL YOURSELF TO HEAL THE RELATIONSHIP

How much healing you need will depend on the level of pain that was inflicted and the kind of trust that was broken. For example, if you find out that your spouse has cheated on you with your best friend, you are going to need some serious healing. This won't happen overnight. It will require time, patience with yourself, and professional help. Again, in situations of infidelity, a counselor is recommended—not only for couple therapy, but also for individual therapy for each party. The person who has been victimized has a lot to overcome emotionally.

Here are some ways you can help yourself in the healing process:

+ Find a support group for the particular experience you are going through. Though there may not be support groups for every kind of trust violation, there are for the major violations, such as infidelity and emotional abuse. Check with your church, a local counseling center, the Internet, or friends who have also gone through trust violations to learn the available resources.

+ Seek individual counseling from a professional Christian counselor.

+ Journal about your experience, your current feelings, and where you want yourself and the relationship to be in the future.

A PERSONAL JOURNAL IS AN IDEAL ENVIRONMENT IN WHICH TO "BECOME." IT IS A PERFECT PLACE FOR YOU TO THINK, FEEL, DISCOVER, EXPAND, REMEMBER, AND DREAM.

—BRAD WILCOX,
AUTHOR AND PROFESSOR AT BRIGHAM YOUNG UNIVERSITY

As you go through the process of healing, avoid bashing the person who broke your trust. Do not go behind their back and begin talking negatively about them because this will prevent you from having a heart of forgiveness. It's okay to talk to one confidant about what happened in order to process your feelings. It's not okay to talk to someone about it for the purpose of condemning the other party or gossiping.

The goal in this final stage is to help you, the victim, see that the relationship cannot be healed unless you are healed. Underlying anger, resentment, and hostility will build a wall between you and the offender. You must pursue ways to heal yourself emotionally and mentally so your relationship can move to a deeper and healthier state.

HITTING THE RESET BUTTON ON THE RELATIONSHIP

It is clear that after a relationship has been broken by trust, you can't just say, "Let's start over," because that won't solve any of the problems or heal the emotional pain. You and the other party need to commit to restore the broken trust. You must both be willing to work through the COME FORTH method together and individually in order to heal yourselves and the relationship. Then you can hit the reset button together as emotionally healthier people who will hopefully be in a better relationship together.

CHAPTER RECAP

For the victim of broken trust, the process of healing and restoration in the COME FORTH method is represented by "FORTH": (1) forgive, (2) open conversations, (3) request what you need to get back to a healthy relationship, (4) talk about the betrayal to a confidant or professional, and (5) heal yourself to heal the relationship.

The case of Rick and Mary is a great example of a couple who used the COME FORTH method and succeeded. Even though Mary was having an affair, Rick wanted to save their marriage, so he confronted Mary with his knowledge of her infidelity. Mary did not immediately admit to the affair or apologize. Instead, she denied the adultery even though she was secretly making plans to leave her husband for the other man.

However, both Rick and Mary sought counsel and advice in the midst of their marital crisis. Having been given time by Rick to think about her marriage, Mary eventually chose to stay with her husband, admit her infidelity, and commit to work to restore the marriage through counseling. Rick and Mary went through a very difficult time, but in the end, it made them a stronger and closer couple. Their marriage is now better than ever. The restoration of the marriage didn't happen overnight. It was empathy, humility, commitment, and apology—the four core elements needed for the restoration of a relationship after broken trust—that made the reconciliation possible.

QUESTIONS FOR REFLECTION

1. Has someone in your family violated your trust? What is the status of your relationship?

2. If you are in a relationship in which trust has been broken and you haven't forgiven the offender or reconciled with them, how can you begin to apply the COME FORTH method to restore the broken trust?

3. What do you personally find most helpful about the "FORTH" portion of the COME FORTH method?

HIDDEN BEHAVIOR #5:

A LACK OF INCLUSION

CHAPTER 10

THE IMPORTANCE OF A SENSE OF BELONGING

When people neglect to include some of their family members in activities, it is a recipe for broken relationships and damaged emotions. Our desire to belong and have interpersonal attachments with others is a fundamental human need. If we don't feel we belong, there can be serious negative consequences, including physical health impacts and a breakdown in our mental well-being.[16]

Members who are not included in family gatherings and activities feel left out and ultimately rejected by their own relatives. Whether someone was born into, adopted into, or married into a family, they are family. Most people are part of a family, but whether or not they are included in that family will determine if they *feel* they belong.

All family members should be treated equally when it comes to inclusion. This concept might seem like common sense, yet many families are failing in this regard. In this chapter, we will look at various reasons why people are not included in family gatherings. We will also explore solutions so that you can be prepared with the tools you need to make your family inclusive, welcoming, and loving.

---

16. R. F. Baumeister and M. R. Leary, "The Need to Belong: Desire for Interpersonal Attachments as a Fundamental Human Motivation," *Psychological Bulletin*, 117, vol. 3 (1995), 497–529.

"THEY ARE NEW TO THE FAMILY AND WE DON'T LIKE...."

One reason certain family members aren't included is that they are new to the family and disliked. Newcomers are sometimes rejected because of their differences or past failings. A handful of friends have confided in me that some of their family members did not attend their weddings or almost didn't attend because those members didn't like the people they were marrying. What an awful way to start a relationship with in-laws! Whether the rejection comes from a mother-in-law, brother-in-law, or anyone else in the family, it is extremely hurtful for the couple to experience before they even walk down the aisle.

Perhaps the family members believe that by boycotting the wedding, they can somehow break up the relationship. I have yet to see that happen. It may have happened with some couples, but in many instances, when family members are waging a war against an engaged couple's relationship, it takes the couple's love and commitment to a new level. They now have something to fight against *together*. It is also a battle to win together, to prove that their love is real and lasting. Even a relationship that may have fizzled can be made passionate again by a parent or other family member forbidding the romance. The heart wants what the heart wants. Telling someone they cannot or should not love someone is like telling them they shouldn't breathe oxygen. Love is hard to fight against. Families who battle someone marrying into the family are only creating hard feelings and strained relationships.

ALL FAMILY MEMBERS SHOULD BE TREATED EQUALLY WHEN IT COMES TO INCLUSION.

Here is a good real-life example of how *not* to act. The names and some details of this story have been changed for privacy reasons. In the chapter on gossiping, we talked about a similar scenario. When Jason got engaged to Megan, his family became very upset. They didn't think Megan was the right choice for Jason because she had previously been married and divorced and he had never been married before. Jason's mother said she didn't believe God would bring her son a woman who had already been married. Against his wishes, Jason's family did a background check on Megan. They didn't find anything that Jason didn't already know. Jason's family also met with Megan's ex-husband to inquire about her. They did this behind Jason's back, but the news of this meeting was revealed through a close family friend.

Jason's mother and two sisters did not show up for the bridal shower, even though they lived near where the event was being held. They chose not to attend out of spite, to show Megan they didn't accept her or the marriage. Their boycott made an impact: Megan felt extremely hurt and rejected by her new family. She was also embarrassed by the absence of Jason's family members at the shower, as guests asked why they were not present. However, the boycott didn't stop the couple from going forward with the wedding.

On the evening of the shower, words were exchanged between Jason and his parents. He blamed them for the fact that the ladies of the family had not attended. They were the ones who were encouraging other family members to behave in this way and ultimately reject Megan.

The day of the wedding, Megan and Jason weren't sure if Jason's family would come. Even though his parents and siblings weren't supportive of his choice of a wife, Jason still wanted them present at the ceremony. It was his wedding day and he desired that his family be by his side. He had asked his brother to be his best man, but his brother had told him just days before the wedding that he couldn't do it because he didn't agree with the marriage. This was extremely hurtful to Jason and caused a break in his relationship with his brother.

Jason and Megan did get married, and they have been married for over fifteen years. Their relationship with Jason's family has never been what they had hoped for. They thought that once they were married, everyone would come around and accept their relationship. The family had said they would move forward on good terms, but they have failed to include Jason and Megan in holiday events to which everyone else in the family was invited. They didn't even invite the couple to the first Christmas gathering after their marriage. Jason's parents, along with his two sisters and their families, have gone on yearly summer vacations together but have never invited Jason and Megan. The family's failure to include the couple has shown their continued rejection of Megan. Although they claimed to have finally accepted her, their actions have spoken otherwise.

YOU'RE GOING TO COME ACROSS PEOPLE IN YOUR LIFE WHO WILL SAY ALL THE RIGHT WORDS AT ALL THE RIGHT TIMES. BUT IN THE END, IT'S ALWAYS THEIR ACTIONS YOU SHOULD JUDGE THEM BY. IT'S ACTIONS, NOT WORDS, THAT MATTER.
—NICHOLAS SPARKS, *THE RESCUE*

BE WELCOMING, LOVING, AND ACCEPTING

How about your own family? Are all the members welcome at events and gatherings, including in-laws and potential spouses? Even though you might not like the individual your relative plans to marry, find a way to accept and appreciate them anyway. Look for the positives in that person and their relationship with your family member. Perhaps the individual was married before and your family member is aware of it. Why is it anyone else's business to hold that against the person?

If you love your family member, then you should show love and acceptance toward whomever they choose to marry. It is their decision, not yours. You never know when the next person a family member brings to your parents' house for dinner or to a family wedding is "the one." Treating each individual they bring home with respect and kindness is how family should act.

It is a shame that "good Christian families" are some of the worst offenders when it comes to rejection through exclusion. Did Jesus meet with only the blameless and sinless while He was on earth? No, He was loving and welcoming to all. He didn't hold people's pasts against them but accepted them into His circle. His example shows us that we should also accept and love others. He instructed us to act in this way. For example, in the book of Matthew, Jesus said the following regarding judging others:

Do not judge, or you too will be judged. For in the same way you judge others, you will be judged, and with the measure you use, it will be measured to you.   (Matthew 7:1–2)

We should keep in mind that God has repeatedly used sinners for His work. He doesn't dismiss people from serving Him or being a part of His family because of their past wrongdoing. For instance, Moses was one of God's greatest servants even though he murdered a man early in life. (See Exodus 2:11–15.) Rahab was a hero doing God's work, and she was previously a prostitute. (See Joshua 2:1–21; 6:16–25.) If God can welcome those who have greatly sinned into His family, then we can learn from His Word and ways.

Frankly, a family that is inhospitable toward newcomers is not being a good family. We should be more than just tolerant of others. We need to be welcoming, loving, and accepting of them, regardless of their past mistakes, socioeconomic status, religion, or any other differences. It is remarkable how, in a society where we are supposed to be tolerant and accepting of diversity in our workplaces and organizations, many people throw out these ideas when it comes to their family members. It is not our place to judge. This releases us from the burden of having to manage the relationship choice of a family member. If we reject their decision, it will only create division in our relationship with them. Accepting their decision because it is *their decision* will foster goodwill and positive communication.

ADDRESS GENUINE CONCERNS

This is not to say you shouldn't talk to your family member if you have legitimate, fact-based concerns about the person they intend to marry. For example, if you know that your future brother-in-law is not being faithful to your sister, take the issue to her with the evidence. You have the right to speak to your loved one about it one time. They only need one conversation to get the message. Tell them you are concerned because you love them and want the best for them. However, do not have this discussion in the presence of their partner. That would be like pouring gasoline on the issue, lighting a match, and throwing yourself into the flames. When someone is in love, they are often oblivious to the flaws of their significant other. Even if they recognize the flaws, they may be dismissive of them or minimize their potential effect. This is because "love is blind." It causes people to lose their ability to think rationally so that they can't see the relationship as clearly as outsiders are often able to.

Therefore, when you share your concerns, expect that your family member will not like what you have to say. They may react negatively toward you and your perceptions of their intended. The things you say may be 100 percent correct, and you have stated them to protect your loved one. However, you will probably find they cannot hear them clearly or in a reasonable way because of their emotional attachment to the other person.

I have witnessed a variety of situations where loved ones have confronted a relative about a romantic relationship. Unfortunately, it has only fractured their own relationship with their family member; it has done nothing to break up the couple's relationship or engagement.

Let me give you an example. Tonya and Phillip were engaged to be married. Tonya was from another country and was considerably younger than Phillip. Phillip's entire family was concerned that Tonya was using him to get a green card to stay in America and that she was also taking advantage of him because of his wealth. They were worried that Tonya would eventually leave Phillip once she had her permanent resident status and enough of his money to live on.

Phillip's brother and adult children went to him directly and voiced their apprehension about the relationship. However, they didn't just communicate their concerns once. They expressed them repeatedly in phone calls and in person. Almost every time Phillip was with his family, they would bring up the issue. They didn't outwardly treat Tonya unkindly, but it was obvious they didn't like her or want her to be around. Tonya could sense this. They weren't inclusive or welcoming of her in the slightest. In their minds, they weren't doing anything wrong because they hadn't cut Phillip out of their lives. But Tonya felt like an outsider, unwanted, and rejected by her fiancé's family.

Phillip wanted everyone to get along so they could be a family together, but he got tired of listening to his relatives' complaints and negativity. His family relationships had become strained. Over the course of several months, he created distance in those relationships. He saw his children and brother less often and stopped calling them. Instead, he drew closer to Tonya.

Phillip and Tonya got married, and they didn't invite Phillip's family to the wedding. Phillip knew how they felt, so it seemed better for the couple to elope and enjoy their wedding alone. They didn't want the negativity from Phillip's children and brother to intrude on what was supposed to be a happy day for them.

After that, there was little contact between Phillip and his family, all because they chose to take a stance against Tonya. They wanted to protect Phillip from being used, but they refused to accept the situation after expressing their concerns. The end result was that Phillip's family lost their relationship with him because of their incessant rejection of Tonya through their words and behavior. Phillip's children no longer had their father in their lives and his brother no longer had his only brother in his life.

WE NEED TO BE WELCOMING OF NEWCOMERS, REGARDLESS OF THEIR PAST MISTAKES, SOCIOECONOMIC STATUS, RELIGION, OR ANY OTHER DIFFERENCES.

The fact of the matter is this: if your family member has chosen to make a commitment to someone they love, then you must accept their decision or you may lose them. Again, you can address the situation once out of concern by having a heart-to-heart conversation with them. However, you should not expect them to end their relationship or even change their mind one miniscule about the person they have chosen to love. They will likely love that person despite the flaws and potential risks you bring up. They will see things differently than you do.

After you have that onetime conversation, tell them that you will love them and be there for them regardless. Then, welcome the person they want to marry and treat that individual with kindness and love. This will enable you to continue your relationship with your loved one. Your main concern should be your relationship with your family member, not their marriage. Remember that you cannot take the blinders off a person in love. The blinders are there by choice. If and when they decide to take them off, their relationship with their significant other may indeed end, but often that doesn't happen until something extreme occurs.

For example, a couple named Matt and Sarah got married. Both of their families had objected to the wedding because they were from different religious backgrounds. Matt also had major financial and legal troubles going into the relationship. Sarah's family had warned her that by marrying him, she would be getting into a financial nightmare. She had told her family that she and Matt would work things out and be just fine financially. Her perception of the situation was shaded by rose-colored glasses because of her love for Matt. The relationship between Sarah and her family became extremely tense because they insisted on repeatedly addressing their concerns about the impending wedding.

After two years of marriage, Matt's financial and legal troubles came to a head and Sarah had had enough. She wanted to turn to her family, but because her relationship with them had been strained before the marriage and almost nonexistent afterward, she didn't feel she could look to them for support. She also didn't want to feel even worse by having her family members say, "I told you so." Her love for Matt was real, as was their marriage, and the way her family had treated their love felt insulting to her.

The harm that occurred in Sarah's family relationships might have been avoided if her relatives had chosen to accept Matt as her husband whom she loved, rather than criticize him and bring up his flaws so often. If Sarah's family had talked with her about their concerns regarding Matt just once and then proceeded to support her, then, when the fallout occurred, she might have reflected on that conversation and known that her family was understanding. She might also have recognized that they had stood by her in her decision to marry Matt, even though they'd had their concerns. But unfortunately for Sarah, that was not the case.

Supportive families are those that can hold the hands of their loved ones even through their bad decisions. That doesn't mean they have to contribute to the bad decisions or play a role in them. For example, Sarah's parents chose not to pay for her wedding. That was their decision. In such a case, there will obviously be hurt feelings. However, if parents can tell their daughter that they will be there for her at her wedding, even though they don't agree with it, and will continue to cherish her, then they are showing love. Loving a family member through their bad choices is not easy, but it can be done. This means you not only need to tolerate the person whom you don't want them to marry, but also learn how to be welcoming and loving toward them, because God calls us to love one another.

HOW TO WELCOME A FAMILY MEMBER'S CHOICE OF SPOUSE

The following are some ways you can welcome someone who marries into your family even though you may dislike them or have concerns about them.

RECOGNIZE WHY YOU STRUGGLE TO LIKE THE PERSON

The first step is to recognize your feelings of dislike for the person and evaluate why you are having these emotions. It is always permissible to have your own feelings. However, it is not always okay to show those feelings, especially if doing so will hurt another person. Talk about your feelings to someone, such as your spouse or a counselor. Process your emotions, but in the end, make the choice to be a good family member and show love and support toward the person your relative has chosen to marry. Give the individual a chance. You might be surprised to find common ground and even develop a positive relationship with them.

GET TO KNOW THEM

Spend time with this new person in the family. Even if they are just a boyfriend or girlfriend, treat them with the same kindness and respect you would if they were a permanent part of the family, because they might be one day. Make a point to get to know them, asking questions that are safe and not overly personal. Ask them about their childhood, where they grew up, where they went to school, and what kind of hobbies they enjoy. However, don't probe about their relationship with your family member. That will not be well-received. They will not perceive you care about them if they get any sort of inkling that you do not accept the relationship. So, don't go in that direction unless they choose to discuss it with you.

One approach is to treat them as if you are talking to your boss's spouse. You want to keep your job, so you will be kind and show interest, yet not be too nosy. If your boss's spouse told you they were part of a college rowing team, you would probably say, "Wow, that's amazing! Tell me more about that experience. It sounds fascinating." Show the same type of interest to the newcomer in your family.

PUT YOURSELF IN THEIR SHOES

Meeting the family of your significant other for the first time is not easy. It can be nerve-racking and stressful. People usually want to be liked and welcomed. They may try hard because they care a great deal about the outcome of your time together. They want to know that the family accepts them. If they feel judged, discounted, or marginalized, they may become defensive. Additionally, your family member may react negatively if you are less than welcoming.

Do your best to imagine what it is like to be in that moment when you meet new or potential family members. Before you ask the person anything, think hard about whether you would want to be asked the same type of question. Kindness, respect, and a hospitable spirit can go a long way toward fostering positive relationships from the outset. First impressions are a two-way street. Make sure you create an atmosphere that shows you want to get to know this person and welcome their presence in the family from the very first second they walk into your life.

KINDNESS, RESPECT, AND A HOSPITABLE SPIRIT CAN GO A LONG WAY TOWARD FOSTERING POSITIVE RELATIONSHIPS FROM THE OUTSET.

LOOK FOR THE POSITIVES IN THEM

You may be struggling with your relative's choice of spouse because you aren't sure what they see in the person. You can easily recognize the individual's flaws and problems. Once again, try to see things from your family member's perspective. What can you identify that is positive and worthy about this person? You can learn to like someone when you want to notice their good qualities. If you are only looking for the negatives, you will most certainly find them. So, change your mindset. Make a decision that you will look for their good points and what your loved one appreciates about them. Scripture tells us, *"Whatever is true, whatever is noble, whatever is right, whatever is pure, whatever is lovely, whatever is admirable—if anything is excellent or praiseworthy—think about such things"* (Philippians 4:8).

INVITE THEM

Include this new person in family activities. If you are having a hard time accepting them, that is all the more reason to spend time with them, get to know them, and build a friendship. As previously noted, family members draw close and bond with one another by making memories together. How can a new member feel they belong if they are never invited to make memories with the rest of the family? If you and several of your siblings are going on a joint vacation, then don't leave anyone out. Invite your brother and his new wife, too, whether you like her or not. She is family and deserves to be part of the memory-making.

Family dynamics are always changing, especially when people marry into the family. So, do your part to accept the change by embracing these new individuals and inviting them to all family activities. Make a point to ensure that they are not forgotten or excluded. It is up to them whether they accept the invitation.

It's too easy to make assumptions about people. Those whom you think would not want to participate in family activities might be just the people who want family relationships the most. They may have a hard time interacting with the family because they don't have good relationships with their own extended family. Teach them how a loving family treats one another by always inviting and welcoming them to family functions.

APOLOGIZE, FORGIVE, AND MOVE FORWARD

If hurtful words and actions have already been exchanged between the family and the newcomer, seek to mend the relationship with apologies and forgiveness. Apologize if you have wronged the other person and forgive them if they have committed a wrong against you. This is the first step toward healing. Don't hold on to the past and how you were hurt because this will only lead to bitterness. Let it go. If you can't seem to do that, pray to God about it. He can help you heal and move forward.

> *Bear with each other and forgive one another if any of you has a grievance against someone. Forgive as the Lord forgave you.*
>
> (Colossians 3:13)

God wants you to love others. Move forward with a heart focused on the desire to get along and have positive relationships for the sake of your family.

TREAT THEM AS YOU WOULD WANT TO BE TREATED

Treating others as we would want to be treated is called the Golden Rule. It is also biblical. Jesus said, *"Do to others as you would have them do to you"* (Luke 6:31).

Scripture calls us to love others as we love ourselves. (See, for example, Matthew 22:39.) Would you want to be treated with bitterness, spitefulness, or even indifference if you were a new family member? Of course not. You would want to be treated with love, respect, kindness, and a welcoming spirit.

We can't control how the rest of the family acts toward a newcomer. However, we have control over our own actions. We may experience pressure from other family members who may not like this person, but in the end, our actions and reactions are up to us. Nobody can force us to act like a jerk. God wants us to treat those who are new to the family with kindness and consideration, regardless of how others may behave.

IF YOU CAN SET A TREND OF TREATING OTHERS WITH LOVE AND RESPECT, YOU MAY CHANGE THE FUTURE OF YOUR FAMILY.

Remember, you are accountable for *your* actions, not theirs. Make your actions count. You may be surprised that other relatives follow your example. Most people want to be good and kind. If you can set a trend of treating others with love and respect, you may change the future of your family. Those who previously felt rejected and unwanted may begin to feel accepted and therefore open up to the possibility of friendship. I truly believe that all it takes is one person to make the change needed to make relationships positive. Life is better for the whole family when its members are kind and loving.

"THEY WOULD HAVE SAID NO ANYWAY"

A second reason why some family members aren't included is that people have decided in their minds, "They would have said no anyway." Do you have a family member or friend whom you have invited to every gathering but they always decline? Then, the one time you don't invite them, do they get upset at you for not including them? In such a case, you may think, "Why should I even ask? You always say no!" You might even have told them this. If so, more than likely, they became defensive at your comment.

The fact of the matter is that people *want* to be invited, especially when it comes to family events. Our loved ones like to feel wanted and included. They may not be able to attend, but they still want to be asked. Never make the assumption that someone can't attend and therefore doesn't need to be invited. That is a relationship mistake that can hurt family members.

It is not wasted time or energy to extend an invitation to someone you don't believe will attend. Even if they live two thousand miles away and you know they probably can't afford to travel to the family's annual Thanksgiving dinner, you should still extend the invitation. You can preface it with, "I know you may not be able to come because it is such a distance, but we wanted to make sure you knew that you were invited for Thanksgiving." It can take only about a minute of your time to invite someone to a family event in an email or text message. The invitation is saying to them that they belong, are welcome, and are invited to be with their family.

Even if a relative says no twenty times in a row, keep extending the olive branch by inviting them. It helps keep the door open to relationships. If you stop inviting them, you are making the assumption that they don't want a relationship or don't care to be part of the family. Please don't make that assumption.

On the flip side, when you are invited to family events, don't always say no either. Make the effort to be with your family. If you continually decline to attend get-togethers, it makes it hard for those extending the invitations to feel like you want a relationship with them. Relationships take time, energy, and effort. If you always have something "better" to do than visiting with your family, the message you are sending is that your life activities are more important than your relationships. You must take some time to be with your family and participate in family gatherings in order to build and maintain relationships. If you are never there for events such as weddings, birthdays, and graduations, how can you expect your family members to show up for your life events? Relationships need to be give-and-take. You attend their events and they attend yours.

Will it always be an equal reciprocation? Probably not. That isn't always feasible. For example, my parents travel to visit us in Texas far more than we travel to Florida to visit them. It is much harder for us, a family of five with three small children, to fly to where they live for regular visits. However, my parents take turns coming to see us when their work schedules allow. They don't often come together because their schedules differ. However, they both make the effort to visit us, and they fully understand that it is more difficult for us to travel. It is this understanding and flexibility that keeps our relationship harmonious and strong.

PEOPLE WANT TO BE INVITED, ESPECIALLY WHEN IT COMES TO FAMILY EVENTS. THEY MAY NOT BE ABLE TO ATTEND, BUT THEY STILL WANT TO BE ASKED.

Although my parents know that we can't make the trip to Florida every holiday season, they always extend an invitation to us when my family plans to get together for Thanksgiving and Christmas. My mom is always saying, "I just want to make sure you know that you are always welcome." She isn't trying to make me feel bad or put me on a guilt trip about not being able to come to the family gatherings. Instead, this is her way of saying that the door is always open, and we are welcomed by my family. That is a wonderful thing to know! What if the day came when those invitations ceased? That would make me feel like I wasn't wanted by my own family. I am thankful for every invitation we receive because my family is saying they want to be around us and would be happy to see us. So, make sure that your loved ones feel wanted at holidays and other times by inviting them to get together.

"THEY EXPECT OTHERS TO PAY"

Another reason someone might be omitted from family gatherings is that, from past experience or supposition, one or more family members think this person will expect others to pay their way. And sometimes people do take on that attitude. When people presume other members of their family will pay for their meal at a restaurant, cover the entire cost of a joint vacation, and so forth, it is a recipe for strained family relationships. Nobody should ever expect someone else to foot the bill for them. If this presumption is being made, it needs to be addressed kindly but firmly.

If you suggest a family gathering, that doesn't mean you must do all the work, pay for everything, or even be the host, for that matter. It can just be an offer to get together. One option is to go to a restaurant. The restaurant doesn't need to be fancy or expensive, just one that everyone can afford and that can facilitate a gathering of your relatives. Another option is a covered dish get-together at someone's home. The extended family on my dad's side is huge. When I was growing up, dinners were always potluck. Every family brought food to share with the entire group. This kind of arrangement takes the burden off everyone because no one person is expected to make the whole meal or host the entire family.

When you are the one extending the invitation, make your expectations clear at the outset. If you want everyone to come to your house for a meal and bring a dish to share, then tell them that up front. If you invite people to go to dinner at a restaurant and want everyone to pay for their own meals, let them know it will be dutch. Just be sure they know what that term means!

There should never be an expectation that a particular person will pay just because they have more money than everyone else. Although that is an assumption people sometimes make, it is a sense of entitlement that has no place in families. You shouldn't expect a handout from another family member, even if that person is incredibly wealthy and you are poor.

If a family member blesses you with dinner, a vacation, or anything else, then you should be grateful. Nobody owes anyone anything. I have friends whose parents pay for their family vacations. They are lucky! However, this doesn't mean I expect my parents to do the same. Every family is different. When those expectations exist, it can lead to hard feelings, resentment, bitterness, and broken relationships. The person who is always paying for everything may begin to feel they are being used. Therefore, develop a mindset that nobody owes anyone anything in your family—from a material standpoint—and you will have better relationships.

Appreciation can go a long way. If you have a generous relative, show your gratitude with both your words and actions. And never expect them to continue to give as they have in the past. Just because you are family doesn't mean that what is theirs is yours, not by any stretch of the imagination. If they paid for your vacation one time, don't assume that they will, or should, do so in the future. You are both adults, and adults are responsible for themselves and their own immediate families, meaning their spouses and the children they are raising. Thus, count your blessings and be grateful for what a family member chooses to give you. Having zero expectations of handouts and being appreciative of any gift, whether it is dinner out, a vacation, or used furniture, will lead to healthy and happy family relationships.

DEVELOP A MINDSET THAT NOBODY OWES ANYONE ANYTHING IN YOUR FAMILY— FROM A MATERIAL STANDPOINT—AND YOU WILL HAVE BETTER RELATIONSHIPS.

Perhaps it is you who are wealthy. You know the Bible encourages us to be generous and God rewards generosity.

There is one who scatters, yet increases more; and there is one who withholds more than is right, but it leads to poverty.

(Proverbs 11:24 NKJV)

Scripture does call us to help with people's needs, but we must be aware that the terms *needs* and *wants* are very different.

But if anyone has the world's goods and sees his brother in need, yet closes his heart against him, how does God's love abide in him?

(1 John 3:17 ESV)

This verse doesn't mean that you must automatically pay for another family member's vacation because you are wealthy and they are not. A vacation is not a need but a want. It also doesn't mean you must always cover your relative's rent when they can't pay it in a particular month. It truly depends on the circumstance. If your brother has problems making rent because he doesn't spend his money wisely or is having a hard time holding down a job due to irresponsibility, then paying his rent may be enabling the behavior. That is merely putting a Band-Aid on the situation. Instead, you might offer to assist your brother in putting his finances in order or finding a new job. Or, if your cousin has an addiction and spends all his money on gambling, drugs, or alcohol, then paying his rent will not likely be helpful in the long run. Don't be quick to throw money at a family problem. The person needs your help with their issue more than they need money for rent. Be part of the solution. Help your loved one to address their underlying problem.

This is not to say you should allow your relative to become homeless and destitute. Family members should always be a safety net for one another. Even if you only have a couch for them to sleep on, then provide your couch so they don't end up in a homeless shelter. Help loved ones when they are in true need, as the Bible has called us to. However, remember that you should never invite someone into your home who may harm you or your family. For example, the issues of addiction are complicated and never easy on family members, so seek professional help in such a case. Your family member's life may depend on it.

"THEY CAN'T AFFORD TO DO WHAT WE DO"

Excluding certain family members because they can't afford the activity—such as going to a nice restaurant—is not kind or fair. I will say this again, just to be clear: creating family gatherings where others are excluded because they cannot afford to be there is wrong.

Suppose one of your brothers wants the entire family to go on vacation to Mexico at an all-inclusive resort, but you have another brother who wouldn't be able to afford the trip. He never finished college, as you and your other brother did, and his job in clothing retail doesn't pay much. He's doing okay financially, but he generally lives month to month and doesn't have extra cash for lavish vacations.

How should you approach this situation? The brother who wants the whole family to get together in Mexico, with everyone paying their own way, should not be attacked for being oblivious to the fact that his brother can't afford the trip. Instead, talk to him and make a more suitable suggestion. Use the "feedback sandwich" method, which we discussed in chapter 5 of this book. This means that you address the problem but sandwich it between two positive statements.

PART OF INCLUSION IS TAKING INTO CONSIDERATION THE LIMITATIONS OTHER FAMILY MEMBERS HAVE. THOSE LIMITATIONS MAY BE EMOTIONAL, PHYSICAL, OR FINANCIAL.

For example, you could say, "I'm happy that you want to plan a family vacation and I appreciate the time you have put into researching this location. However, I am concerned that our younger brother might not be able to go on the trip because he can't afford it. Would you be willing to consider a different location that has a variety of cost options, such as a resort that has camping on the premises? I realize this may change our destination, but I was hoping we could include everyone. I am so thankful that you came up with the idea of doing a vacation together. I am happy to help research other locations."

When some family members continually choose to gather in places that are too expensive for others, it makes those who can't afford it feel unwanted. Part of inclusion is taking into consideration the limitations other people have. Those limitations may be emotional or physical, not just financial. If you are thinking of planning a vacation to Hawaii for the whole family, but one of your family members has a fear of flying and would never be able to get on an airplane, then that person would be excluded.

Inclusion is purposeful. When you want to include all family members on a vacation, you intentionally consider each person and determine whether it would be realistic for them to participate. You look at the cost, distance, and dates of the vacation. You might not be able to give everyone their first preference, but you can do your best to make the trip as feasible as possible for everyone.

I WANT TO TAKE THE WORD CHRISTIANITY BACK TO CHRIST HIMSELF, BACK TO THAT MIGHTY HEART WHOSE PULSE SEEMS TO THROB THROUGH THE WORLD TODAY, THAT ENDLESS FOUNTAIN OF CHARITY OUT OF WHICH I BELIEVE HAS COME ALL TRUE PROGRESS.... I GO BACK TO THAT GREAT SPIRIT WHICH CONTEMPLATED A SACRIFICE FOR THE WHOLE OF HUMANITY. THAT SACRIFICE IS NOT ONE OF EXCLUSION, BUT OF AN INFINITE AND ENDLESS AND JOYOUS INCLUSION.

—JULIA WARD HOWE, POET, AUTHOR, AND ABOLITIONIST

Keep in mind that just because not all of your relatives can afford a more expensive trip, that doesn't mean you can never go on a nice vacation with your immediate family or friends. Plan your own vacations according to your personal preferences and plan your extended family vacations in a manner that is inclusive of all. A cruise might be a good option for a family trip because there are a wide variety of prices available based on room selection. Some interior state rooms can be relatively inexpensive. I have gone on cruises with extended family where, because we were all from different income levels, we each chose accommodations we could personally afford. With these arrangements, we were still able to dine together, go to the pool together, and see the same shows. The only difference was our individual rooms. In most cases, we also chose four-night or five-night cruises because it was unrealistic to expect family members to be able to get away for two full weeks or even one week. People felt included because the trip wasn't a lavish, fourteen-day cruise that cost more than their car.

Although we purposefully planned these vacations to make them affordable for everyone, for various reasons, some members could not join the rest of the family on the trips. You must realize that it is next to impossible to coordinate schedules so that every family member is able to go on every trip. However, the goal is to be as inclusive as possible by endeavoring to make choices and selections that work for everyone. Then, each member can decide for themselves if they are able to go. Your job as a good family member is to try to be as inclusive as possible.

CHAPTER RECAP

Practicing inclusiveness in a family may seem like common sense. However, there are good families that forget this very basic principle, causing certain members to feel unwanted when they are left out. When newcomers marry into the family, it is especially important to be welcoming. This is when relationships are first developing, and making someone new feel wanted is crucial to having good family relationships. Additionally, our relationship with an existing family member can be destroyed when their new spouse or significant other is not made to feel welcome.

The key to being inclusive is asking. If you don't ask someone to participate, then you haven't included them. For example, when only a few members of the family go on a vacation together and neglect to invite the others, it can make those other members feel left out. Always invite everyone; it is up to each individual whether they participate. There are creative ways to make sure everyone is able to afford and enjoy joint family activities.

QUESTIONS FOR REFLECTION

1. Was there ever a time when you were not included in a family gathering? What happened? How did it make you feel?

2. Do you include all your family members at gatherings where the whole family is supposed to be invited? Why or why not?

3. What can you do to be more inclusive of your family members and build better relationships with them?

CHAPTER 11

HOW TO CULTIVATE A WELCOMING ATMOSPHERE

The exclusion of family members is not always intentional or acknowledged. This is why it is a hidden behavior that has the potential to destroy a family if it is never addressed. Sometimes, inclusion means getting back in contact with family members we've inadvertently neglected and reestablishing those relationships. Other times, it means strengthening the family ties we have already begun to develop. We can accomplish both of these goals by cultivating a welcoming atmosphere. Let's look at some ways to do this.

RECOGNIZE THAT RELATIONSHIPS AND INCLUSION REQUIRE TIME

To build relationships with extended family, you need to spend time together. If you only see family members every ten years, it is difficult to have good, healthy, close relationships. Emotional distance can occur when you never see one another in person. The relationships become much more like online connections. If you have a social media account, then you probably have friends who comment on your postings quite often. Online, your relationships appear interactive and close. However, when you come together in person with an online friend, you may sense there is something missing. If you haven't also developed a face-to-face relationship, the online connection lacks true substance. There is a level of interaction that happens in person that cannot occur with electronic communications.

Sending messages via social media, email, or text is simply less personal. That is exactly why it is easier for people to make comments online that they would never say to someone in person. They can hide behind the screen. Most of the time, face-to-face interactions and time spent together are essential for building relationships that are genuine and deep.

Of course, there is nothing wrong with keeping up with family and friends through social media. However, this should not be the only source of your interactions. You must make the effort and take the time to meet in person because it will provide the opportunity for shared experiences and true interpersonal connection. This is what is needed to create bonds and memories with others.

In the past few years, I have helped both of my brothers plan their weddings. Much of our communication was conducted via email, text, and phone calls. This planning was a shared experience, but the real connections were made in person when the weddings were held. The time we spent together decorating, playing cards, and of course attending the marriage ceremonies themselves provided opportunities for great bonding. Our time together at these wedding weekends forged the deeper relationships we enjoy today.

FACE-TO-FACE INTERACTIONS AND TIME SPENT TOGETHER ARE ESSENTIAL FOR BUILDING RELATIONSHIPS THAT ARE GENUINE AND DEEP.

TAKE THE INITIATIVE

Have you ever lamented over the fact that a relative seldom or never gets in touch with you? Years ago, I was complaining to my mom that a family member never seemed to call me. She lovingly pointed out that phones work both ways and I could call that person. She was right. If we want a relationship with someone and they never call, email, or text us, then the ball is in our court! There are no rules when it comes to who initiates contact.

Similarly, when I was first married, I thought it was up to my mother-in-law to contact me. I don't know exactly why I thought that way, but I know I am not alone. I have heard other ladies complain that their mothers-in-law never call them. They, too, expect their husbands' mothers to be the ones to initiate the relationship. This is erroneous thinking. Let me reemphasize that if you want closer bonds with the people in your family, then you need to take the initiative. Be the one to make the effort. Even if it has been years since you were in contact with a family member, there is no better time than the present to reestablish a relationship.

Let me offer this caution: if you are going to contact a family member because you want a relationship, don't try to sell them something at the same time. This seems to be a trend in our society. Every week, I get contacted by long-lost friends and family members on social media. I have received a multitude of messages from people I haven't heard from in years. Of course, the messages are always upbeat and positive, appearing to show genuine interest in my life. But typically, the senders aren't reaching out because they want a real relationship. Once I reply, the conversation soon turns toward whatever they want me to purchase.

There has been a rise in multilevel marketing businesses, and many people are becoming involved in them to pursue home-based income. However, if you sincerely want to resume contact with someone and you have such a business, avoid discussing your business or finances. Nothing will turn people off quicker. They will become highly suspicious of your motives when money becomes a topic of discussion.

SHOW GENUINE INTEREST IN THE OTHER PERSON

Sometimes, even though we want a better relationship with a family member, we don't know how to get started. The best way to initiate a relationship is to show interest in the other person. You might begin with a phone call. Don't call to tell them all about your life and what you have been doing for the past five years. Just let them know that you have missed them and want to be in touch more often. Then, ask them about themselves. Show you are interested in their life and desire to know them better.

If making a phone call to a family member you haven't spoken to in more than a year seems too intimidating or awkward, then start smaller.

You could mail them a short note of greeting. Or, you could begin following them on social media. Show interest in their postings. Make comments on their family activities. Knowing what is going on in their life via social media will also give you more to talk about when you are ready to make the phone call.

Here's how making an initial connection through social media might work. You may have a sister-in-law whom you feel bad about never calling. What makes it harder is that your families haven't gotten together in several years. You want to be inclusive and have a relationship, but you think it would be uncomfortable to just call her out of the blue. So, you sign up for her favorite social media platform and start following her. You arrange your settings so that her news comes up every time she posts something.

Soon afterward, you learn that her son was elected class president and her daughter is doing competitive cheerleading. You wouldn't have known these things if you hadn't followed her on social media. You make supportive comments on both posts. Your sister-in-law is a great cook, and a few days later, she posts a recipe for a baked chicken dish she recently made that looks amazing. You'd like to try it, but you have a question about whether to use a glass dish or metal pan, so you text her and ask for advice. From there, texting becomes a regular occurrence between the two of you. The door to a relationship has opened.

Within a month, you arrange to have a phone call to discuss the upcoming Thanksgiving holiday, and you make plans for your families to get together. It all began because you took the first step to initiate contact and interaction through social media. You kept the relationship progressing by communicating via texts and a phone call, and now your family will spend a holiday together after years of being apart.

FAMILY MEMBERS ARE TYPICALLY THE PEOPLE WE ARE LINKED TO THE LONGEST IN LIFE, SO DON'T MARGINALIZE THOSE RELATIONSHIPS BY PUTTING THEM ON THE BACK BURNER.

There can be many variations of this scenario. If you live close enough to your family member to meet, then you can ask them to get together for coffee or a meal. Make time to forge those relationships because you need family. We *all* need family. Life is short. People are precious. Take the opportunity to get to know those whom God connected you to when He placed them in your family. These are typically the people we are linked to the longest in life, so don't marginalize family relationships by putting them on the back burner.

KEEP YOUR COMMUNICATIONS POSITIVE

As mentioned previously, it's important not to call a relative merely to talk about your own life. However, it's especially important not to contact them just so you can *complain* about your own life and the way things are going for you. It isn't fun being with someone who makes you feel awful after spending time with them. Thus, there is no point in trying to make a connection with a family member if you only call them to grumble. Before contacting them, think about your motivation. If you tend to complain or talk negatively, then you need to retrain your thoughts and behavior. Don't say anything at all unless you have something good to say.

One way to help yourself stay positive is to jot down a few notes about constructive topics to discuss. For instance, you could ask the person about their children or latest vacation. You could congratulate them on their new job. Having your list on hand will provide you with options for redirecting the conversation if it turns negative. Obviously, you can't control what the other person says, and they might have a negative attitude. However, you can set the tone of the conversation by keeping your own words positive.

You will find that family will want to take your calls and forge relationships with you when you show interest in them and your conversations are uplifting. It is all about feelings. When they hang up the call, if they feel good, then they will be likely to pick up the phone the next time you call. But if you tend to be negative and leave your loved one with a depressed feeling, then you are conditioning them to avoid you.

Think about it in this way: do you get an "icky" feeling every time you see a certain person's name appear on the caller ID of your phone? Try to determine why you react that way. There is likely something about your experience with this person that makes you feel sour toward them. Perhaps they are a perpetual complainer who causes you to feel depressed, or a continual bragger who makes you feel insignificant. Whatever it is, you feel bad when you talk with this person, so your gut reaction is not to answer their calls. You want to avoid that feeling.

Know that your family members may have the same reaction toward you if you are the one who is the complainer or bragger. They *will* begin to avoid you. People want to be around others who make them feel good, lift them up, and leave them with an overall sense of well-being. Therefore, if you find that someone is avoiding you or not returning your phone calls, you need to assess your behavior—especially if multiple people seem to be reacting in this way. Ask yourself, "What is this person's experience when they spend time with me? Do I leave them feeling good about themselves or do I leave them with a sour pit in their stomach?" You must be objective when you reflect on your interactions with a loved one who has been avoiding you.

Don't remain wondering about the situation if you can't figure it out on your own. If you don't think you are being a negative influence, yet a family member still seems to avoid you, there is always the option of writing them a note or attempting to meet with them in person (perhaps through the help of a third party in the family) and respectfully asking why they aren't taking your calls or accepting your invitations to get together. Don't go to them with an attitude of confrontation. Instead, take a calm and gentle approach, seeking to learn what you may be doing to offend them or put them off. In this way, you are more likely to receive an honest answer. Let them know you want to understand so you can improve your interactions, not only with them but also with others. We are not always aware of personal habits that unintentionally put others off. Sometimes, we don't know unless we ask.

PEOPLE WANT TO BE AROUND OTHERS WHO MAKE THEM FEEL GOOD, LIFT THEM UP, AND LEAVE THEM WITH AN OVERALL SENSE OF WELL-BEING.

Prepare yourself to hear something you may not like. Self-improvement usually involves facing a flaw so that we can work to change it, for our sake as well as the sake of others. The information you receive from the person can help you better yourself and your relationships. Take time to digest what they have to say before responding. Then, simply thank them for their thoughts and honest opinion. After you talk with them, do some research on how you can change the negative habit or improve the behavior that is driving people away.

I don't believe there is anyone who is completely unlikeable. It is our behaviors that make us unlikeable, not who we are in our core being. God only makes good creations. If your sin nature has overtaken some aspect of your personality, then you may have adopted behaviors that turn people away. I have an example of this from my own life. As previously mentioned, I participated in scholarship pageants while I was in high school and college. It was a great way for me to earn tuition for college. However, as I became more involved in this endeavor, I grew a bit self-centered.

Pageants are all about highlighting your positive attributes, whether physical or otherwise. It took me a little while to realize that I was putting people off because I was constantly talking about myself. I would bring up the foundation I started, my voice lessons, my scholastic achievements, my gown fittings, and whatever else was happening with my pageant preparations. I was working toward becoming a better person so I could compete and earn scholarships. But because my focus was so inward, I was oblivious to how others felt when they were around me. I admit it was a vain time in my life. I'm grateful that I recognized it was a problem and learned to become humbler by focusing on others more than myself. Instead of talking about my life, I turned my attention to other people's lives. I learned to hold back my incessant talk about pageants by becoming more interested in what was going on with those around me.

Do you have difficulty developing long-lasting friendships, or are your relationships with your family members usually strained? As I learned in my life, talking about yourself can come across as bragging, so don't fall into the trap of thinking you are simply discussing positive topics when you might really have an issue with vanity. Instead of focusing on yourself, talk with others about themselves or other subjects in an optimistic, uplifting manner. If you want your family to feel loved, wanted, and included, you must show it through your conversations and actions. This is not a onetime event either. You need to develop a healthy habit of treating family members and others with consideration and interest when you are around them.

OFFER PRAISE AND ENCOURAGEMENT

Another way to cultivate a positive atmosphere is to offer praise and encouragement to others. Look for ways to honestly compliment your family members when you are around them. In fact, this is what Scripture teaches us to do:

> *Therefore encourage one another and build each other up, just as in fact you are doing.* (1 Thessalonians 5:11)

> *And let us consider how we may spur one another on toward love and good deeds, not giving up meeting together, as some are in the habit of doing, but encouraging one another—and all the more as you see the Day approaching.* (Hebrews 10: 24–25)

If positive thoughts about someone cross your mind, don't just brush them off. Instead, speak those words of affirmation and praise the next time you see them. It will help them to feel uplifted while they are in your company. You want them to know they are loved, to feel empowered, and to have the sense that they are doing something right in the world. Even the smallest of compliments can go a long way toward accomplishing this.

LOOK FOR WAYS TO HONESTLY COMPLIMENT YOUR FAMILY MEMBERS WHEN YOU ARE AROUND THEM.

I was on a camping trip with my sister Natalie, and she complimented me on an article I had recently written. It meant a lot to me. She provided me with specific examples of how the article had helped to reshape some of her own thoughts and behaviors related to parenting. Knowing that my own family was reading my articles and taking them to heart gave me a boost of confidence in my writing. Natalie might have read the article, taken it to heart, and never mentioned it to me. However, she acted in the loving way that a friend or family member should by telling me that she benefited from my advice.

BEING INCLUSIVE STARTS WITH "I"

Becoming an inclusive family starts with each individual member. We can't expect others to be inclusive if we ourselves are not acting in that way. Again, when just one person is willing to make the effort to start implementing the principles of inclusion, they can set the trend of having a welcoming spirit in their family. The following is a checklist of ways all of us can work to provide inclusion within our own families:

- ✓ Invite every member to family events, whether they are married or single, and whether or not they have children.

- ✓ Take into consideration accommodations for those with disabilities. For example, if one family member is in a wheelchair, then don't select a venue or home for family gatherings that is not accessible. If another member doesn't drive at night, plan lunchtime get-togethers.

- ✓ Set the cost expectations low for any gathering that involves all family members and the need to spend money. For example, if one sibling has a McDonald's budget and two other siblings have the means to go to a five-star restaurant, offer a compromise. Ensure that the restaurant choice allows for the inclusion of the sibling who has the lower budget. You might offer to pay for that sibling's meal, suggest an inexpensive restaurant, or host the gathering in your own home. Any of those options would help to make the gathering inclusive for all.

- ✓ Avoid any language that is derogatory toward a particular race or ethnicity. (We will discuss this point further in the next section of this book.) You may have extended family members who come from diverse backgrounds. Be sensitive to others and never say anything that could be offensive regarding their culture or other differences. Most families are a melting pot of backgrounds. Be cognizant of this fact and accept everyone as the unique human being God made them to be.

✓ Be warm, inviting, and accepting of all family members. If you feel unwelcoming toward certain members, they will sense that tension from you. Again, evaluate your negative feelings, let go of them, and look for the positives in people. Family tensions do not foster a loving or inclusive atmosphere.

✓ Do what you need to do to heal any past hurts and restore relationships so that hostility and resentment are not present at family gatherings. Inclusion means making everyone feel wanted and accepted. When family members are invited only out of obligation and not out of a genuine desire to spend time with them, then inclusion is not taking place. If previous or ongoing conflicts are causing ill will between family members, then the parties involved should address these situations and work toward reconciliation. That way, when family members are invited, they will genuinely feel included and wanted because the issues have been resolved.

✓ Be self-aware of assumptions, judgments, or biases that can harm your relationships with others. For instance, if you assume that someone does not want to attend family functions because they never call you, you could be making a false conclusion. They may not call often because they have young children and it is hard to talk over the noise and chaos within their home. This doesn't mean they don't want a relationship with you. It just means they have a home environment that makes phone conversations difficult. Instead of presuming, give people the benefit of the doubt. When you need to know something, simply ask the person so you can have clarification.

✓ Be respectful and compassionate toward all family members, especially those who are experiencing difficulties in life. For example, if you have a sibling who is going through a divorce, when you see them in person, don't simply pretend the situation is not happening. Provide emotional support when you come together, being sensitive to their privacy and the best timing for asking how they are doing. They may feel like an outsider if everyone in the family acts as if nothing has changed in their life. Family members need to be able to count on their loved ones for encouragement and support.

✓ Raise your children to be inclusive. This means treating all people with dignity and respect regardless of differences, including race, age, gender, religion, income, abilities, and sexual orientation. For example, when you see that your daughter and her girl cousins are not including the boy cousins in their play, and the boys want to play with them, you need to help them see they need to include the boys too. Let them know that excluding others is not okay. Teach them to accept all who want to participate. Exclusion also often happens among children when there are age differences. Teach your older children they need to include their younger family members. Your teaching methods can incorporate asking questions such as "How would you feel if you were being left out?" or "How do you think they feel when you don't allow them to play with your group?" Train your children to be inclusive from your own example as well.

✓ Be willing to speak up and say something when someone is being left out. Appeal on their behalf to let others in the family know you believe in inclusion for the sake of the entire family and all the relationships involved.

Remember, we are all responsible for our own actions. We can't point fingers and say that others are the sole cause when a family member is being excluded. We must be willing to stick up for those who are being left out. Each of us can help to make an excluded family member feel welcome and loved. The impact of your acceptance of someone who feels rejected and unwanted by your family can be life-changing.

THEY MAY FORGET WHAT YOU SAID—BUT THEY WILL NEVER FORGET HOW YOU MADE THEM FEEL.
—CARL W. BUEHNER,
A GENERAL AUTHORITY OF THE CHURCH OF JESUS CHRIST OF
LATTER-DAY SAINTS AND GUBERNATORIAL CANDIDATE

CHAPTER RECAP

Relationships are a two-way street. Nobody should expect another person to be the one to initiate a relationship. As an adult, you are responsible for yourself and for fostering relationships with your family members through regular contact. Some tips for cultivating a welcoming atmosphere are: recognize that relationships and inclusion require time, take the initiative, show genuine interest in the other person, keep your communications positive, and offer praise and encouragement.

Becoming an inclusive family starts with each individual member. We can't expect others to be inclusive if we ourselves are not acting in that way. When just one person is willing to make the effort to start implementing the principles of inclusion, they can set the trend of having a welcoming spirit in their family.

QUESTIONS FOR REFLECTION

1. Have you lost contact with an extended family member with whom you would like to renew a relationship? Are you waiting for them to initiate contact? Why not call or write them a note today to reestablish communication?

2. What is the general tone of your conversations with your family members? Is it positive or negative? Do you talk mainly about yourself or do you show genuine interest in the other person and their activities? If you tend to be negative or self-focused in these conversations, what can you do to change this habit the next time you talk with a family member?

3. How might you offer genuine praise and encouragement to a family member this week?

HIDDEN BEHAVIOR #6:

A FAILURE TO ACCEPT DIFFERENCES

CHAPTER 12

WHEN DIFFERENCES DIVIDE FAMILIES

Another significant issue that is causing the breakdown of extended families is a failure to accept one another's differences. The United States, like many countries, is becoming more culturally diverse. When people reject others who are different from them, it causes misunderstandings and conflicts, some of them severe. Unfortunately, such conflicts are becoming more prevalent in our world.

When rejection due to differences occurs among the members of a family, it causes similar misunderstandings and conflicts. As a result, people feel unwanted and unloved. I am referring to the rejection an individual feels because their family does not accept them *as a person*. Families get hung up on differences and choices they may not agree with, without recognizing the larger considerations, and this causes strife and division. We can't expect our loved ones to agree with all our choices and decisions. However, we do expect our family members to love us as human beings, just the way we are, right where we are in life. When we sense we are not loved at the most basic human level, then we feel alienated from our families.

GOD MADE EACH OF US UNIQUE

Acceptance of others is one of the greatest forms of love. No two people were made the same. Every person is an individual creation of God our Father. This is by His perfect plan and design. He wanted us all to be unique, which is why each of us is different from everyone else.

> *But now, O LORD, you are our Father; we are the clay, and you are our potter; we are all the work of your hand.* (Isaiah 64:8 ESV)

> *For you formed my inward parts; you knitted me together in my mother's womb. I praise you, for I am fearfully and wonderfully made. Wonderful are your works; my soul knows it very well.* (Psalm 139:13–14 ESV)

> *For the LORD sees not as man sees: man looks on the outward appearance, but the LORD looks on the heart.* (1 Samuel 16:7 ESV)

A family *can* change its dynamic from not accepting differences among its members to accepting those differences. To make the transition, the members need to learn tolerance and respect for one another. Again, does that mean we have to agree with everyone else's choices and preferences? No, but it does mean we are willing to back off from judgmental tendencies and to love without setting conditions for acceptance.

In this chapter, you will find guidelines for creating good relationships with all your family members as you love them unconditionally, just as Scripture commands us to. The Bible doesn't say to love others *if* they think like you do, parent like you do, or make the same lifestyle choices you do. No, it simply says to love one another. In fact, Scripture tells us to love others with intention *"because love covers over many sins"*:

> *Above everything, love one another earnestly, because love covers over many sins.* (1 Peter 4:8 GNT)

> *Be under obligation to no one—the only obligation you have is to love one another. Whoever does this has obeyed the Law.* (Romans 13:8 GNT)

My children, our love should not be just words and talk; it must be true love, which shows itself in action.   (1 John 3:18 GNT)

Be always humble, gentle, and patient. Show your love by being tolerant with one another. Do your best to preserve the unity which the Spirit gives by means of the peace that binds you together.

(Ephesians 4:2–3 GNT)

ACCEPTANCE OF OTHERS IS ONE OF THE GREATEST FORMS OF LOVE.

GUIDELINES FOR CREATING GOOD RELATIONSHIPS

People naturally gravitate toward those who are similar to themselves. We all tend to like being around others who are like us. We also have a better understanding of who they are because we understand ourselves. However, when someone is our complete opposite in outlook and personality, it is difficult for us to understand their motivations and decisions. For example, if you are a devout Baptist who lives in the suburbs and your sister embraces atheism and lives on a commune, you are not going to experience life the same way or see eye to eye on much. Having a relationship with a sister who has a completely different set of beliefs and values is not easy. However, not only is it possible to have a relationship with her, but you can have a great one. The following are practical tips for building relationships with members of your family who are different from you.

DON'T TRY TO CHANGE PEOPLE

First, let go of trying to change your loved ones. When you continually make suggestions to a family member for change or improvement, you communicate that you don't accept them for who they are. You are essentially telling them they are not good enough. It is not your job to change anyone. You don't have the power to do that. It is up to the person to decide whether to change. Every additional comment you make that reflects your desire for them to change causes disintegration in the relationship.

BE AN ENCOURAGER

Rather than trying to change people, become their encourager. If you have a hard time being around a particular relative, but you want to have a relationship with them, then always be looking for their positive qualities. Instead of being quick to judge and offer criticism, let the words of your mouth be pleasing and uplifting. Seek ways to constructively compliment them. Offer affirmative feedback and be supportive when they are going through a difficult time. You will find that a positive attitude from you will likely produce a positive response from the other person.

Remember, the process of changing a behavior is most successful when you replace the old behavior with a new one. Working on accepting others who are different than we are is not easy. However, it can be done. Start implementing this positive behavior even before you are around your family members. Retrain your brain to look for the good in them. Whenever a criticism about an individual comes to mind, immediately try to replace it with a sincere compliment. Then, speak that compliment directly to the person the next time you see them. You may be amazed at how it can change your relationship. You can get along with almost anyone if you can be genuinely pleasant with them and seek to notice their good qualities.

If you can't think of anything nice to say, then you aren't looking hard enough. There is good in every person. Look for three positive attributes in them. Praise what is good. Resist all temptation to provide criticism or suggest any kind of change. If you make a mistake and accidently say something negative, then apologize immediately and return to focusing on the positive.

CHECK FOR HEART ISSUES

Seeking to see the good in our relatives should be standard policy in all families. Then, why are we are often quick to see the negative? As we discussed in the section on criticism, one of the biggest reasons is that we have developed contempt for a family member. Contempt is a hardness we allow to grow in our heart due to feelings of anger or bitterness. Its presence means there is some pain from the past that we have not forgiven and released.

When we harbor contempt against someone, we are much quicker to find their faults. We continue to build contempt in our heart when we act on it, such as trying to change a family member through negative feedback and criticism. Although we might temporarily feel better about ourselves when we put this person down, the long-term effects are negativity in our own heart and damage to the relationship. You may need to examine your heart to uncover any contempt that has grown there from past hurts. If you can identify it, you can work to change it.

BRING UP ANY CONCERNS IN LOVE

If contempt is not at the core of your desire to change a family member, it could be something completely the opposite. You deeply love that person and want the best for them. You observe that they may be going about matters in their life in the wrong way and want to help them correct their course. They may be caught up in a sin that is harming themselves or others. There are biblical guidelines for bringing up such issues with our family members, as we have discussed in detail in chapters 2 and 10. I encourage you to review these chapters so you can talk over your concerns with them in a loving and constructive way.

Suppose you discover that your brother is having an affair and is planning to leave his wife, and you want to talk to him about this issue. Use biblical guidelines, offering practical solutions for his situation that you have researched ahead of time. Then, at the end of the conversation, let your brother know you will be there to listen, and you want to help him with his marriage. Most importantly, tell him that you will love him regardless of the decision he makes. God doesn't tell us to cut off our family members when they make mistakes or decisions we don't agree with, especially ones that are not wrongs against us personally. Yes, God's Word does tell us to help a loved one who is sinning by talking to them about their sin. However, once you have done your job of talking to them, leave it alone. Continuing to bring up the same issue is pointless. It is also not helpful to your relationship with your family member. God commands us to love one another, and loving a relative under difficult circumstances means loving the sinner in spite of their sin.

However, don't do anything that causes you to take part in their sin. *"Keep watch on yourself, lest you too be tempted"* (Galatians 6:1). This means that if your brother wants to leave his wife because he desires to shack up with his new girlfriend, and he asks for a loan to help him pay for his divorce attorney, you don't loan him the money. If you know the funds are going to be used for something that is displeasing to God and outright sinful, then you shouldn't provide them. You don't have to be nasty about it or act holier-than-thou. Simply saying no is enough.

You will still love him as a brother. You will still invite him for Christmas dinner, as you always have. If he is divorced by that time and has a new girlfriend, then you invite the girlfriend too because what is done is done. It is not your life. It is *his* life and *his* decisions. You cannot make your brother change. Neither can you force him to make the right choices. Keep your eyes focused on your own life. If you aren't certain whether you should be helping a family member who may be in a sinful lifestyle, then go to a trusted pastor or Christian counselor and ask for guidance. You don't have to make these decisions alone.

If you follow this guideline, you will unburden yourself. When you don't have to harp on your brother about his failing marriage every time you speak with him, your load is lifted. You can provide advice if he asks for it. But if he doesn't ask, it's likely because he already knows your thoughts and opinions based on your previous conversation about it. You may want something better for him, and you may want to see his marriage survive, but you can't force that to happen.

Release yourself by giving up the need to try to change others in your family. You will thank yourself in the long run. The relationships with your loved ones will likely improve as well. Remember that you can always continue to pray for them.

HURTING RELATIONSHIPS CAN BE HEALED WHEN OUR DESIRE TO CHANGE PEOPLE IS REPLACED BY OUR LOVE AND ACCEPTANCE OF THEM.

In the long run, trying to change your family members is like trying to herd cats! Don't bother. Cats refuse to be herded and people don't like to be told they need to change. As mentioned previously, the best way to improve relationships is to look for the positives in other people, especially in those whom you want to change. You will see relationships take a 180-degree turn when people who felt judged and condemned now feel loved and accepted.

Realize that progress won't happen overnight. Damage that has already been done can't be repaired instantly. However, your consistent changed behavior will shift the dynamics over time. Hurting relationships can be healed when our desire to change people is replaced by our love and acceptance of them.

STOP TREATING PEOPLE LIKE OUTCASTS

People can sense when others don't like them or are judging them. In order to build good relationships with our family members, we can't keep treating them like outcasts. Remember that retraining your brain is very helpful for stopping judgmental and condemning thoughts. Your behavior and words will be transformed as you proactively replace negative thoughts and attitudes with positive ones. First and foremost, however, change begins in the heart, with a desire and decision to love others unconditionally.

Is it your intention for everyone in the family to be treated with loving-kindness, and for nobody to feel rejected or outcast? You may need to express that intention in words before following up with consistent behavior that proves your intention. Tell your family members, especially those who may feel rejected, that you want everyone to get along and you are going to work on promoting an accepting atmosphere in the family. You may not be able to change the mindset of all your family members, but you may influence some by your new resolution and behavior.

As we discussed in the previous section of this book, one way to help family members move from feeling rejected to feeling loved is to include them in family activities and events. Often, those who feel like outcasts in the family feel that way because they actually *aren't* being included in family affairs. Perhaps they are not being invited to family dinners and holiday celebrations. That trend can change with you. You have the ability to invite people to family functions and activities, especially the ones that you host. Make a point to do so. Set the example of inclusion so that you don't have a single family member who feels like an outcast. Everyone desires to be asked to an event; it makes them feel wanted. Even if they say no each time you ask, you are doing your job as a loving family member by extending the invitation.

DON'T THINK OF PEOPLE AS LESS THAN YOURSELF

If you think you are better than someone else, you will likely project those thoughts through your actions and perhaps even your words. You may never have admitted out loud to a family member that you believe you have made better life choices than they have and therefore are a better person. However, they may be picking up on those attitudes. Two ways to change this situation are to show respect and steer away from sarcasm.

SHOW RESPECT

The Scriptures instruct us to love others as we love ourselves. For example, Jesus said,

> *The second most important commandment is like this one* [loving God with all our heart, soul, and mind]. *And it is, "Love others as much as you love yourself."* (Matthew 22:39 CEV)

When we treat others as we want to be treated, we are showing them respect. It is very difficult for people to feel accepted and part of a cohesive family unit if they don't feel respected. For example, perhaps you have a brother-in-law who has a hard time holding down a job and has been fired from multiple positions. Poking fun at his inability to keep a job or making little jabs about how he always lacks money because he is unemployed is less than respectful. It is unkind and rude to him as a human being.

In an earlier chapter, I mentioned that we should treat an in-law or potential in-law with the same courtesy we would treat our boss's spouse. Here is a similar approach I have followed and recommended for many years: you should treat family members as you would treat a stranger in a checkout line. If we can be friendly and engage in small talk with a total stranger in a store, then why can't we do the same for members of our own family? Showing common decency, kindness, and respect go a long way. So, even if you can't think of a specific compliment to say to a relative, then at the very least, treat them with the same courtesy you would offer another person in a public place. General pleasantries can go a long way to helping people get along.

There are no ifs, ands, or buts about treating our family members as we would want to be treated. This means we don't only treat them with respect *if* they treat us with respect as well. Clearly, we cannot control other people. We can only control ourselves. Therefore, be a good example in your family by treating others with kindness and respect, even if it is not reciprocated. You will foster a more loving family environment, whether or not you feel like you are making a difference.

You never know the impact your kindness is having. The ripples of your positive behavior can create additional ripples of kindness within the family. Each drop of kindness and respect you give to fellow family members will spread outward. The effect will be their own improved attitudes toward other family members and a positive experience of being together. Positivity breeds positivity. When people are continually treated with loving-kindness, they will learn to reflect the way they are treated. The change may not be instantaneous, but over time, you will notice the beneficial effect.

> REGARDLESS OF WHO YOU ARE OR WHAT YOU DO,
> IF YOU ARE LOOKING FOR THE BEST WAY TO REAP
> THE MOST REWARD IN ALL AREAS OF LIFE,
> YOU SHOULD LOOK FOR THE GOOD IN EVERY
> PERSON AND IN EVERY SITUATION AND ADOPT
> THE GOLDEN RULE AS A WAY OF LIFE.
> —ZIG ZIGLAR, AUTHOR AND MOTIVATIONAL SPEAKER

STEER AWAY FROM SARCASM

A major way some family members express disrespect is through sarcasm. If you have a tendency to make sarcastic remarks, make sure you never direct them toward your loved ones. I'm not referring to good-natured teasing, because that is a way some families interact and express affection. However, even here we need to be careful. What one person considers a joke, another person may consider a put-down. We must learn how each family member responds to teasing remarks.

Sarcasm is often a disguised insult. For example, suppose your sister serves a dish of cold mashed potatoes because she got sidetracked in family conversations and forgot to reheat the dish for the meal. You say to her, "No problem, we all wanted to have cold mashed potatoes for dinner." Your sarcasm is an insult masked as humor. You might get a chuckle, depending on your tone and ability to deliver the sarcasm. However, the core intent of the message was an insult. There was no need to express the comment. It was made as a way to put your sister down.

Once more, you will need to retrain the way your brain works so you can learn to treat your family in more affirmative ways. If, out of habit, your initial reaction to a family circumstance is a sarcastic thought, then hold yourself back from commenting. Instead, use that moment to think of something positive to say. It may not feel natural to you at first, but new habits often feel unnatural because we aren't used to them. Practice over time will make compliments and positive feedback seem more natural.

BE A GOOD LISTENER

Another vital guideline for creating an accepting atmosphere in the family is to be a good listener. Family members often feel rejected if they sense nobody is listening to them. How can someone feel like a part of the family when none of the other members are really communicating with them and don't seem to care what they think? For example, they may feel rejected when their phone calls are never returned or their comments during conversations at family gatherings are cut short.

Remember that we can make someone feel they are not fully accepted or included when we become a "conversation hog." When you call a family member, do you take time to ask them what is happening in their life? Do you sincerely want to know how they are doing? Are you interested in the current events in their life? People pick up on these vibes. They won't think you actually care about them if you spend the entire conversation talking about *your* job, *your* house, *your* husband, and *your* amazing children. If you aren't asking questions but spend most conversations talking about yourself, then you are not being a good listener.

Let me be frank: if we don't listen when we talk with our family members, then we are failing in those interactions. Good listening skills are paramount to making our relatives feel accepted and wanted.

Suppose your sister asks how your kids are doing and you tell her that your daughter won her school spelling bee. Your sister replies by saying that her daughter always excelled at spelling at that age and then goes into a long-winded story about her daughter's achievements. You are probably going to think she doesn't really care about your daughter or the news you shared because she launched right into talking about her own daughter without even offering any congratulations. However, this might not actually be the case. She might simply have poor listening skills.

We *all* need to develop good listening skills and use them with our loved ones. Having these skills will make us better communicators and foster positive family relationships. When we become good listeners, we show that we care enough to hear what the other person has to say. We give them the opportunity to share about their own lives, demonstrating that we are interested in what's happening to them and their families.

In addition to showing that we care, allowing people to talk about themselves gives them the opportunity to open up to us. Are there any people in your family who might feel unaccepted? Engage them in conversation and ask open-ended questions that indicate you want to get to know them. Then, make a point to listen to them. Often, people who feel unaccepted also feel misunderstood or judged. Involving them in conversations and using attentive listening skills can be like a healing balm to a wound in their life.

LISTENING IS A MAGNETIC AND STRANGE THING,
A CREATIVE FORCE. THE FRIENDS WHO LISTEN
TO US ARE THE ONES WE MOVE TOWARD.
WHEN WE ARE LISTENED TO, IT CREATES US,
MAKES US UNFOLD AND EXPAND.
—KARL A. MENNIGER, NOTED PSYCHIATRIST

As people are given the opportunity to talk, it is important that they don't think their feelings are being disregarded or they are being looked down on. They want to be loved and accepted by their family, and they may desire an opportunity to share some of their inner thoughts and feelings. Don't let personal judgments or the particular moral decisions you have made for your own life prevent you from showing acceptance to another human being, especially someone in your extended family. If they don't feel loved by their own family, then who can they rely upon to feel accepted and wanted?

Because the art of listening is so essential to strong family relationships, the next chapter will focus on how we can show acceptance to the members of our family through specific listening skills.

CHAPTER RECAP

The Bible tells us to love one another: *"Above everything, love one another earnestly, because love covers over many sins"* (1 Peter 4:8 GNT). Repeated attempts to change people can convey the message that we don't accept them the way they are or that they aren't good enough. We need to show love to our family members and demonstrate tolerance toward them, especially those who may be very different from us. This doesn't mean we agree with them regarding all their life choices, preferences, and opinions. It does mean we are willing to treat them without judgment or condemnation and look for their positive qualities. Some guidelines for creating good relationships are the following: don't try to change people, stop treating people like outcasts, don't think of people as less than yourself, and be a good listener toward others.

QUESTIONS FOR REFLECTION

1. Was there ever a time when you felt judged by another family member? What happened? How did it make you feel?

2. In what ways could you show more respect toward a particular family member?

3. What guideline or principle in this chapter resonated with you the most? Why? How might you put it into practice to help create a more accepting family?

CHAPTER 13

HOW TO SHOW ACCEPTANCE THROUGH GOOD LISTENING SKILLS

Our ability to listen to others plays an instrumental role in our interactions with them. The website MindTools says, "Listening is one of the most important skills you can have. How well you listen has a major impact on your job effectiveness, and on the quality of your relationships with others."[17] When we learn to be better listeners, we can improve the quality of all our relationships, especially those relationships with family members who feel left out due to their differences with others in the family. You can help your family members to feel loved and accepted by taking the time to truly hear and affirm them.

Let me encourage you that effective listening skills can be learned by people of any age and stage in life. It's never too late to become a better listener! Here are some strategic ways to show acceptance toward others through listening.

LOOK THE PERSON IN THE EYES, NOT AWAY FROM THEM

If you are having a one-on-one conversation with someone, keep your focus on them by looking them in the eyes as you talk. Have you ever been out to dinner with a family member or friend, trying to have a nice time,

---

17. "Active Listening: Hear What People Are Really Saying," MindTools, https://www.mindtools.com/CommSkll/ActiveListening.htm.

but the person won't make eye contact with you? They are continually looking over your shoulder at the activity of other patrons in the restaurant or perhaps at a television screen on the wall, and you are unable to gain their full attention. When this happens, it is frustrating and irritating because what this person seems to be nonverbally communicating is that they don't care what you have to say or even that you are present. You can be left feeling superfluous and disconnected from them.

Making regular eye contact when you talk with people shows that you are fully engaged in listening to them. As the conversation progresses, resist the temptation to become distracted by other activities in your environment that may seem more interesting. If the person is important to you, and you desire a relationship with them, then sustaining your attention is a way you can convey that they matter to you more than what is happening around you (even though those activities may indeed be more interesting to you!). Pay attention to the individual and focus on what they are trying to communicate.

YOU CAN HELP YOUR FAMILY MEMBERS TO FEEL LOVED AND ACCEPTED BY TAKING THE TIME TO TRULY HEAR AND AFFIRM THEM.

PUT TECH ASIDE FOR THE TIME BEING

Many of us are losing the human connections that are right in front of us because we are continually focused on personal technology. Our relationships with those closest to us are suffering because we spend more time looking at our smart phones than actually interacting with our loved ones. For example, you might be deep in conversation with your spouse when your phone buzzes. You check to see if an important (or merely interesting) message has come in. When you take that moment to look at your phone, you are disrupting the flow of the conversation. Your spouse may feel that others who are not actually present in the room are more important to you than they are.

The same principle applies to all our relationships. If we keep checking for messages on our phone or using the Internet when we are with our family members, we are nonverbally communicating that other contacts and activities take priority over them. We need to start being more attentive to those who are present with us. When we are having a conversation with someone we love, we should ignore the urge to look at our phone every few minutes or whenever we hear the buzz or beep of a notification. If your phone allows you to check the amount of your daily usage, start paying attention to that number. How many hours a day are you spending active on your phone? Is this time you are taking away from your family or friends? Should the phone be put down or turned off for longer periods so you can focus your attention fully on those who are most important in your life?

AVOID INTERRUPTING AND CUTTING OFF

We live in an era when life seems to be in fast-forward. The level of busyness causes us to feel rushed in our daily activities. And when we are busy and feeling rushed, we hurry through our conversations. This leads to negative behaviors like interrupting and cutting off our loved ones when they speak. I know that I am guilty of this behavior.

Getting three kids out the door for school in the mornings can be hectic. Every day, there seem to be problems that slow us down and threaten to keep us from being ready on time. Five minutes before we are to leave, my son might get a bloody nose that stains his shirt, so we need to change his clothes. Or, my daughter might suddenly remember that it's "Crazy Hat Day" at school and we need to hunt for a silly hat for her to wear.

I hate being late, so when I'm rushing around in the mornings, especially those mornings when bigger problems arise, I tend to become more blunt and impatient in my communications. When my husband or one of my children asks a question, I tend to cut them off or finish their sentence for them. For example, if my husband asks what we're having for dinner that evening, I might snap back, as I walk in the other direction, "I don't know and I don't have time to think about it now since we are running late."

Many of us feel *most* rushed when we are at home with our families, particularly in the mornings and evenings. Our good listening skills deteriorate when we are overbooked, overworked, and harried. But a lack of listening at these times can have a significant negative effect on our relationships. We must start becoming more conscious of the busyness that causes our conversations to be cut short. When we interrupt our loved ones, the nonverbal communication we express is that our own words are more important than what the other person has to say. They conclude that their words don't matter to us and their feelings get hurt.

We have to take the time to slow down and listen. If we have something very important ahead of us, such as a job interview or a boss awaiting our arrival at work, then we should calmly explain the situation to our family members so they understand why we need to make the conversation brief. If we aren't in a rushed situation, then we don't have an excuse to interrupt our loved ones while they are speaking. Doing so is discourteous and shows that we aren't fully listening.

When you allow the other person to finish their thought, you are exhibiting good listening skills. You are also communicating that you care about their thoughts and feelings. Whether you are talking to your five-year-old child, your husband, or your eighty-year-old chatty aunt, it is important to listen without cutting them off or interrupting. Fully listening demonstrates your love and care for them.

Of course, there are times when you may need to set limitations if someone has been talking for a long period of time and you have important responsibilities to fulfill elsewhere. You can gently let the other person know you've enjoyed talking and would like to continue the conversation in the future and then excuse yourself.

Let me challenge you to take note of how many times you interrupt or cut people off as you go through a busy day. Interrupting others is a negative habit that you can make yourself more aware of in all your conversations so you can begin to change your behavior.

WE MUST START BECOMING MORE CONSCIOUS OF THE BUSYNESS THAT CAUSES OUR CONVERSATIONS WITH OUR FAMILY MEMBERS TO BE CUT SHORT.

LISTEN FOR UNDERSTANDING AND DON'T MAKE ASSUMPTIONS

As we listen to our loved ones speak, we need to try to put ourselves in their shoes to understand their perspective. This means resisting the temptation to make assumptions and instead hearing them out completely. Making assumptions can cause conversations to shut down, and in the end, we fail to understand our family member's viewpoint.

For example, suppose you will be going on a weeklong family vacation with your siblings and their families. You know that hiking is a favorite family activity, and you want everyone to go on hikes together every day to enjoy the scenery of the beautiful location where you all will be staying. So, you plan out a different hike for each day, mapping it all out in advance. When you arrive at the vacation spot and your family members get together the first night for dinner, you excitedly tell them about the hikes you have planned. Your sister gives some pushback, stating, "I don't know if all the kids can handle it." Instead of letting her finish her thought, you cut her off by saying, "Well, my kids are the youngest in the group, and I know they can do it." You say this rather curtly because you have invested a lot of time and energy into the planning of these daily hikes. You assume she made the objection because your kids are young, but you know they will be able to handle it because they have done similar hikes in the past. You can tell that your sister may have more to say, but you are thankful she doesn't object any further because you want the hikes to happen as you had anticipated.

The next day, everyone participates in the hike. You believe this first outing was a success because everyone got to enjoy the striking scenery and time together. However, the following day, your sister says she is not going and neither is the rest of her family. You don't protest because the others are waiting to begin hiking and you feel there isn't time for a lengthy conversation. Your sister and her family skip the hike the next day also.

On day five of the trip, you learn that your sister's eldest son is still recovering from a previous knee injury. You now recall that he had a bad accident during a basketball game a few months back. Now you must have a conversation with your sister because you had forgotten about your nephew's injury when you were planning the hikes. You need to apologize for failing to be sensitive to his needs so that he could be included in all of the activities. Your sister explains that she wanted to tell you that first night at dinner, but you had obviously worked so hard on the plans that she didn't want to hurt your feelings, offend you, or start an argument. She says that her son tried the hike the first day to see if he could do it, but unfortunately his knee swelled up, and it has been swollen and hurting ever since.

Your refusal to let your sister finish her thought and remind you about your nephew's injury shut down the conversation, caused hurt feelings, and had a negative impact on your family trip. If you had allowed her to complete what she wanted to say, you would have understood the situation from her perspective. If one of your kids had been dealing with a knee injury, you wouldn't have planned the hikes. You might have substituted a different activity, such as canoeing or kayaking.

Knowing that you should have listened to *actually hear* what your sister wanted to say, you now feel guilty for ruining your nephew's vacation. Including him in the activities was far more important than any hike. You had been upset that your sister and her family hadn't been participating in the outings, but for four days, you had failed to ask why they didn't want to go. Your curt response to your sister at the dinner table the first night, when she conveyed that not all the kids might be able to do the hike, made her feel like you didn't care what she had to say.

The vacation would have gone a lot better if you had listened carefully and tried to see things from your sister's perspective, rather than making assumptions about her thoughts or motivations. Those assumptions got you into a situation where you now need to ask for forgiveness.

MAKING ASSUMPTIONS ABOUT OUR FAMILY MEMBERS CAN CAUSE CONVERSATIONS WITH THEM TO SHUT DOWN, AND IN THE END, WE FAIL TO UNDERSTAND THEIR VIEWPOINT.

GIVE NONVERBAL CUES

While listening to someone, it is vital to give nonverbal cues to show you hear and understand what they are saying. If you are having a conversation with someone and their face exhibits no expression, it is hard to determine whether they are actually comprehending your words. I speak to groups, and when I am trying to explain something but all I get in return are blank stares, it frustrates me. That's when I feel I have to ask, "Do you know what I mean?" Many people don't realize that their nonverbal skills fall flat!

If you have ever spoken to a crowd, did some people sit with deadpan expressions, giving you no indication whether they liked or understood what you were saying? Then, were there others whom you were drawn to look at while you spoke? If so, this was likely because they were demonstrating good listening skills. They were exhibiting facial expressions that showed they related to what you were saying, were in agreement, or appreciated your message. They may have often smiled or nodded, which is probably what caused you to look in their direction in the first place. You knew that these particular people were truly engaged with what you had to say.

No matter what the setting, if people fail to give us nonverbal communication through facial expressions or body language when we are speaking, it becomes difficult to make a connection with them. You can't feel connected with someone when you have no idea whether they love your thoughts or think they are ridiculous.

Therefore, when you are listening to someone else speak, especially a loved one, remember this point and make sure to use positive, nonverbal cues. You want them to know that you hear and care about what they have to say. Again, a few good ways to show you are listening and comprehending include nodding your head in agreement, smiling, or making other facial responses that correspond with what you are feeling during the dialogue. Of course, keep in mind that your expressions should match the tone of the conversation. If your cousin is telling you that her dog just died, you don't want to be smiling! A compassionate look and a hug would be appropriate nonverbal communications in such a circumstance.

SHOW INTEREST BY ASKING QUESTIONS

If you want to convey to anyone that you are interested in them, ask them questions about themselves. Most people don't have a problem talking about themselves because that is what they know best in the world. You show that you care about their life by asking about their job, their family, and their hobbies. You can do the same when you get together with your extended family members. As we have discussed in previous chapters, ask questions that aren't too personal or probing, unless you have already established a close relationship. It is always safer to ask general questions.

The best kind of questions are those that are open-ended. Questions that only require a one-word response, such as yes or no, aren't helpful for opening up conversations. Questions that begin with the words *how* and *what* are much more beneficial for getting a dialogue going. Here are some examples:

- How are things going at work?
- How are you doing?
- How are your kids doing?
- What have you been up to lately?
- How was your recent vacation?
- What do you have planned for your next vacation?

Remember to avoid questions that are nosy and intrusive. If you pry too deeply, you will likely receive those one-word answers, showing that they want to end that line of questioning. For example, if you ask your brother, "How is your son doing in school?" and his response is, "Good," then it's probably best to leave it at that, especially if your brother isn't usually prone to one-word answers. If he had something he wanted to share, he would have said it since you provided the opportunity. So, take the hint and change the subject.

Filter your questions through kindness. Think to yourself, "Would I like to have someone ask me this question?" Suppose you and your husband had a rough patch a few years back and you went to marriage counseling and were able to resolve your issues. Now, every year during the holidays when you see your aunt, she asks, "How is your marriage doing?" Being asked that question every single year seems intrusive and prying from your point of view. The quality of your marriage is not your aunt's concern since your relationship with her isn't close.

What you choose to share with your family members about your own life is up to you. You may be family, but that doesn't give anyone the right to know all your business. Just because someone asks a question doesn't mean you need to answer it. You can give the same courtesy to others.

STOP DEBATING AND TRY TO FIND COMMON GROUND

Researchers Jack Zenger and Joseph Folkman reported their findings on good listening skills in the *Harvard Business Review*. They learned that the best listeners—those in the top 5 percent—built up the self-esteem of the person they were communicating with.[18]

I have a handful of friends and acquaintances that I can clearly identify as being in the top 5 percent of listeners. There is one friend with whom I can talk for hours on end. After our time together, I always feel better about myself because she listens to me and has a way of building me up. I have also observed her doing the same with others. She has a positive attitude and finds moments in each conversation to genuinely compliment whoever she is talking with. She does this so easily and naturally that it is obvious her brain is conditioned to look for the positive in others. My friend is a pleasure to be around, and even when she disagrees with what someone is saying, she does so in a friendly, kind, and diplomatic manner that makes her very likeable to everyone. Her ability to engage in positive interaction and disagree in such a nonjudgmental and fair manner helps to make her a great communicator.

THE BEST LISTENERS BUILD UP THE SELF-ESTEEM OF THE PERSON THEY ARE COMMUNICATING WITH.

Remember to look for the positive qualities in people as you listen to them. When you consistently help others feel better about themselves by building up their self-esteem through genuine compliments, you, too, will be perceived as a great communicator.

Zenger and Folkman also reported that the ability to be a cooperative conversationalist is what makes a person a great listener. The top 5 percent

18. Jack Zenger and Joseph Folkman, "What Great Listeners Actually Do," *Harvard Business Review*, July 14, 2016, https://hbr.org/2016/07/what-great-listeners-actually-do.

of communicators in their study were able to have conversations and voice their opinions without putting others down or making them feel bad about their differing opinions.

> Poor listeners were seen as competitive—as listening only to iden-
> tify errors in reasoning or logic, using their silence as a chance to
> prepare their next response. That might make you an excellent
> debater, but it doesn't make you a good listener. Good listeners
> may challenge assumptions and disagree, but the person being lis-
> tened to feels the listener is trying to help, not wanting to win an
> argument.[19]

Getting together with family shouldn't be a time when anyone is trying to win debates. That leads to ill will and dissention between those on opposite sides of the argument. Suppose you have a brother who likes to debate politics every time you get together, but you feel nothing construc-tive comes out of these conversations. In his mind, your brother is trying to win the political debate to prove your ideas are wrong and his views are right. He may think that winning the debate will win you over politically. You feel like you have to continually defend your beliefs. You don't want to be on the defensive every time you get together with your brother, but it seems like your values are being insulted at worst and marginalized at best.

Your brother's confrontational conversational tactics are conditioning you to not want to be around him at all. If his behavior continues, you will likely avoid seeing him as often, perhaps to the point of skipping some family gatherings. You may not even fully recognize why you don't want to be around him; you just know that you feel bad afterward.

If we don't want our family members to feel the same way about us, we need to steer clear of controversial topics and seek common ground instead. Avoiding debates that drive wedges in family relationships is important to keeping those relationships caring. Debating often causes people to feel judged. When they sense they are being judged, they won't feel accepted. The family shouldn't be a source of condemnation and judgment but of love and acceptance. The rest of the world will judge. Family should be a safe haven from negativity and condemnation.

---

19. Ibid.

Therefore, keep debates out of family gatherings and interactions, or at least keep them to a minimum. Let me repeat this famous quote, which provides great wisdom regarding this issue: "They may forget what you said—but they will never forget how you made them feel."

The way we make people feel is paramount to what we say or do. Great communicators know how to make others around them feel valued, respected, and important. We need to convey to our family members that they are of great value to us. We can do this by being good listeners, identifying the positives in them, and affirming them while in conversation.

ALLOW PEOPLE TO HAVE DIFFERENT OPINIONS THAN YOURS

We can keep debates to a minimum by allowing people to express views that are different than our own. Again, one surefire way to make people feel unaccepted in the family is to put down or disregard their opinions. Everyone is entitled to their own opinion. They might be wrong, and so might you. You are each coming from your own vantage point, based on your life experiences and perspectives. We need to be willing to allow others to voice their opinions.

For example, if your family has a strong background of belonging to the Republican Party and the majority of the members are Republicans, then those family members who are devoted Democrats might feel rejected if they are admonished for their beliefs rather than being allowed to express their views. Suppose you have an extended family member who is a staunch Republican or Democrat, and they voice their opinions on social media loud and clear. You come from the opposite viewpoint, and when you respond to one of their postings giving a different opinion of the issues, they lash out at you online and question how you can possibly think the way you do. This sort of reaction makes it personal. They are questioning your ability to think rather than debating the politics in a civil manner. Our best response when a family member expresses a different view is to say, "Thank you for your comments. You are entitled to your opinion and we may never see eye to eye, but that's okay. We're family, and I love you!"

When family members put one another down because they have opposite opinions or viewpoints, making it personal, their relationships will disintegrate and dissolve. But when they refuse to belittle each other for expressing their opinions and instead agree to disagree while still show-ing love toward one another, their relationships can be strengthened. Remember, we are all entitled to our own views. That doesn't mean our loved ones must agree with us. It does mean we are allowed to have our opinions and voice them in a calm and rational tone of voice for the con-sideration of others. They can disagree, but it should be done in a manner that is respectful. So, allow your family members to have their own views about parenting, politics, religion, and more. Listen to them with respect and not judgment. They can have their convictions and you can have yours.

WISDOM IS THE REWARD YOU GET FOR A LIFETIME OF LISTENING WHEN YOU'D HAVE PREFERRED TO TALK.
—DOUG LARSON, NEWSPAPER EDITOR AND COLUMNIST

CHAPTER RECAP

The quality of our listening skills has an impact on all our relationships. Utilizing good listening skills to help others feel accepted and wanted will serve to develop positive family relationships. When we have poor listening skills, we provide little feedback, leaving people uncertain about whether we hear and comprehend what they are saying. Or, we give negative feedback, indicating we don't care or we reject them because of their opinions.

Good listening habits can be learned by people of any age and stage in life. It's never too late! Effective listening skills include the following: look the other person in the eyes, not away from them; put tech aside for the time being; avoid interrupting and cutting off; listen for understanding and don't make assumptions; give nonverbal cues; show interest by asking questions; stop debating and try to find common ground; and allow people to have different opinions than yours.

QUESTIONS FOR REFLECTION

1. Which of the listening skills in this chapter are you regularly putting into practice? Can you give an example?

2. Which skills are you currently lacking? Have you noticed any negative consequences from this lack? If so, what are they?

3. Which of the listening skills can you begin to work on to improve your relationships with extended family members?

CHAPTER 14

WHEN ALL ELSE FAILS, YOU MUST SET BOUNDARIES

We teach people how they can treat us by what we permit them to do. Therefore, if you have a family member who is constantly wronging you, then you have taught that individual you will allow them to behave in that way toward you. As we have discussed, not *wanting* them to treat you in a certain way and not *allowing* that treatment are two different animals. If you don't want to be wronged any longer, then talk to the person and let them know you want the behavior to stop. Tell them that if they persist, you will limit your time around them. Establishing consequences for the negative behavior will have a better chance of achieving results than simply telling them you don't like the way they are acting. That is why, when all else fails in trying to remedy the situation and restore the relationship, you must set boundaries.

It is okay not to be around your extended family all the time. Some families refuse to change. Some families are toxic. A lot of this has to do with family leadership. How do the heads of the family (usually Grandma and Grandpa) behave toward one another and everyone else? The way they treat the other members of the family matters. They are the role models, whether they want to be or not, and everyone is watching them. Do they set a good example of how to treat one another with love and kindness? If not, then the relationships under the heads of the family will probably not be healthy either.

GIVE PEOPLE A CHANCE TO CHANGE FIRST

Before you make the decision to put boundaries in place and see your family members less often, make sure you have given them a chance to change. Take the time to address the issue following the biblical guidelines we've discussed in this book. If the person has been committing a sin against you but is also a believer in Christ who understands the concept of needing to repent for sinful behavior, you can follow the process Jesus instructed us to use in Matthew 18. If the person is not a believer, you will need to use a modified version of the process.

> If your brother sins against you, go and tell him his fault, between you and him alone. If he listens to you, you have gained your brother. But if he does not listen, take one or two others along with you, that every charge may be established by the evidence of two or three witnesses. If he refuses to listen to them, tell it to the church. And if he refuses to listen even to the church, let him be to you as a Gentile and a tax collector. Truly, I say to you, whatever you bind on earth shall be bound in heaven, and whatever you loose on earth shall be loosed in heaven.
>
> (Matthew 18:15–18 ESV)

Since this method is vital for restoring relationships, but may still end with the need to set boundaries, it will be helpful to review each stage of the process before we look at some additional considerations for working through family issues and creating boundaries.

1. GO TO THE PERSON PRIVATELY

The process begins by going to the person privately. However, remember that in cases of physical or sexual abuse, or where you suspect the person may become violent, *never* go to the person by yourself. Don't place yourself or others in a potentially harmful situation. Instead, bring in a professional who knows how to protect everyone involved. For these situations, let me refer you again to the National Resource Center on Domestic Violence, whose website is https://nrcdv.org.

For other types of situations, you can address the person directly. Many times, we are understandably angry about their offense against us. But rather than discuss the issue, we cut the person off. We stop talking to them and make no effort to restore the relationship because we feel self-righteous in our anger. Yet, even if we've been wronged, God wants us to make peace if possible.

> *If it is possible, as far as it depends on you, live at peace with every-one.* (Romans 12:18)

God has called us not only to make peace with others but also to fully forgive them. If we don't speak to a family member about an issue and simply cut off the relationship, then we aren't even trying. Give yourself some time to cool down and allow your anger to recede. Don't feed the anger with thoughts about how much this person has hurt you and how wrong they were. Instead, take the anger to God and ask Him to help you forgive your family member in your heart so you can approach them with the goal of restoration. You can't force someone to apologize to you, but you can give them the opportunity to make things right. All we can do is our part and continue to pray about the situation. The rest is up to the other person.

Suppose your sister continually lies to you. As you follow the process in Matthew 18 of first going to her about the matter privately, use this passage from Galatians as a guide for the manner in which you should approach her:

> *Brothers, if anyone is caught in any transgression, you who are spiritual should restore him in a spirit of gentleness. Keep watch on yourself, lest you too be tempted. Bear one another's burdens, and so fulfill the law of Christ.* (Galatians 6:1–2 ESV)

YOU CAN'T FORCE SOMEONE TO APOLOGIZE TO YOU, BUT YOU CAN GIVE THEM THE OPPORTUNITY TO MAKE THINGS RIGHT.

You need to approach your sister in gentleness as someone whom God loves deeply. This means not only desiring that your own relationship with her be restored but also that she be restored in her relationship with God. When you bring up your sister's wrongdoing, it should be done in a manner that is loving and not condemning. Ask her to cease lying to you because it is destroying your relationship with her and hurting you. To help bear her burden, you might suggest the names of some respected counselors you have researched with whom she could talk about why she has fallen into this pattern of lying, and offer to go with her if she would like you to. If she apologizes and promises to change, then you can proceed with your relationship. If she refuses, then you need to take the next step.

2. BRING OTHERS WITH YOU

When addressing offenses in this next stage, it is best to include one or two members of the family or others who are witnesses to the sin that is being committed against you. Thus, when you talk with your sister again, you might approach her with your parents if they have been present when she has told you lies. If no family members have been present when the lying has occurred, you might still ask those who are aware of the situation to be there. Or, you might ask one or two trusted mutual friends or mature believers whom she knows to accompany you.

3. TAKE IT TO THE NEXT LEVEL

If your sister still refuses to apologize or change, the next step is to *"tell it to the church"* (Matthew 18:17). In the first century church, this meant going to priests or elders. You might go to her pastor or church elders if you feel they would be able to help. In this way, you would be appealing to the spiritual leaders she has already chosen to guide her. These leaders might refer you to a Christian counselor, or as mentioned earlier, you might research a counselor yourself to whom you and your sister could go together. Today, there are Christian counselors who are equipped to handle family conflict. If your sister isn't a Christian and is not open to Christian counseling, you might suggest going to another family counselor to work through the situation.

You can't force your loved one to attend a counseling session, but you can at least make the effort and go through the steps to try to rectify the relationship. The rest is up to them. When you take it to the levels of intervention that involve other witnesses and professional help, it shows your loved one you are serious about the problem and truly desire restoration. You still may not be able to get them to change, but you have a good chance of making a difference in your relationship and setting it up for positive transformation.

4. CREATE EFFECTIVE BOUNDARIES IF NEEDED

The point of this whole process is to give a family member who continually wrongs you the opportunity to make the relationship right and also be restored to God. If, in the end, they refuse and continue to sin against you—lying to you, deceiving you, gossiping about you, or attacking you with verbal or physical abuse—then Jesus said you can treat them as *"a Gentile and a tax collector"* (Matthew 18:17). In Jesus's day, tax collectors were well-known for skimming off the top. In addition, they collected tax money from the Jews on behalf of the Roman Empire, and the Jews despised the Romans. Tax collectors were considered collaborators, and they were excommunicated in terms of social interaction with the rest of the population.

The audience Jesus was speaking to in Matthew 18 did not spend their free time with tax collectors. No "self-respecting" Jew would go to dinner with them. Jesus did, though! However, this passage says they were to treat people who refused to listen when confronted with their wrongdoing as *they* would treat Gentiles or tax collectors, by not associating with them. This is how I apply the teaching in this passage to family relationships: if someone refuses to stop committing sins *against you personally* after you have gone through the steps of trying to restore the relationship, then you can cease spending time with them. God doesn't want His children to be hurt by the sins of others. If someone is blatantly wronging you through their sin and they decline to change, then you can set boundaries, including cutting them off.

However, this does not necessarily mean cutting them off forever. If the person comes to you later and apologizes, while demonstrating they truly are committed to making things right and restoring the relationship, then you need to move forward and also forgive them if you have not already done so. Remember that Jesus told us to forgive even if we are sinned against repeatedly:

> *Then Peter came to Jesus and asked, "Lord, how many times shall I forgive my brother or sister who sins against me? Up to seven times?" Jesus answered, "I tell you, not seven times, but seventy-seven times."*
> (Matthew 18:21–22)

DECIDE HOW MUCH INTERACTION YOU WANT

Please keep in mind that each situation is unique and needs to be treated with careful consideration of the circumstances and people involved. You might no longer have a personal relationship with a family member but maintain a familial relationship. It doesn't have to be an all-or-nothing approach. You can still see the person, but the contact doesn't need to be frequent. You decide how much interaction you want with this individual and what level of closeness you desire for the relationship.

Suppose your cousin embezzled money from the business you ran together. She would not own up to her sin and never tried to apologize or repay the money she stole. Instead of refusing to ever see or speak to her again, you dissolve your business ties with her and create distance in your relationship, thus setting boundaries that will protect you from future abuse. However, there will still be family gatherings such as weddings, graduations, and funerals that both of you will attend. At those events, you treat her with kindness and love because Jesus tells us to love our enemies.

> *You have heard that it was said, "Love your neighbor and hate your enemy." But I tell you, love your enemies and pray for those who persecute you, that you may be children of your Father in heaven. He causes his sun to rise on the evil and the good, and sends rain on the righteous and the unrighteous.* (Matthew 5:43–45)

This means we are to act toward our enemies with respect and civility, still wanting what is best for them. Therefore, whenever you see your cousin at a family occasion, you don't refuse to speak to her. Nor do you bring up the matter of her embezzlement around the other family members. You refrain from gossiping behind her back because that would be a sin on your part. Instead, you smile, greet her warmly, and ask how she is doing.

However, even though you show love and kindness to her, this doesn't mean you must start doing business with her again. Continued boundaries are necessary when someone refuses to stop sinning against you or to acknowledge their wrongdoing. Someone who steals money from you is sinning against you. Someone who physically or emotionally abuses you is sinning against you. Someone who spreads lies about you to others is sinning against you.

It is not easy to handle a situation in which someone sins against you and refuses to make things right or even apologize. We need to understand it's okay to have boundaries with such a person because we must exercise common sense and protect ourselves from being harmed. If someone beats you severely every time you see them, are you supposed to continue the relationship and endure the beatings? Of course not. You are to avoid putting yourself in a position where the person can abuse you.

EACH SITUATION IS UNIQUE AND NEEDS TO BE TREATED WITH CAREFUL CONSIDERATION OF THE CIRCUMSTANCES AND PEOPLE INVOLVED.

Don't allow others to sin against you repeatedly. Again, except in cases of physical or sexual abuse where you always bring in trained professionals to intervene from the start, follow the sequence outlined in Matthew 18, giving people the opportunity to repent and change their behavior. But if all those efforts fail to make a difference and they refuse to change, remember that you are allowed to create boundaries and distance.

Perhaps the dynamics of your entire extended family are toxic. People swear at one another and insults abound whenever you are together, and there doesn't seem to be any hope for change. In this case, you can decide you will only see your family members perhaps two or three times a year. If you feel that dining together at a restaurant would keep everyone better behaved, you can arrange to hold your family gatherings at a public place.

Or, maybe your uncle doesn't approve of the way you are raising your children. He thinks you are too soft on them, and he doesn't hold back from telling you what he thinks you are doing wrong in your parenting style. He also picks on your children, calling them sissies. If you have already expressed your concerns and told him that you won't be able to spend time with him on a regular basis if he continues to talk in this way to you and your family, but his behavior persists, then follow through with your warning to limit contact. You may need to remind him before your few scheduled visits that conversations need to stay positive. Again, having clearly communicated consequences is important to defining how you will allow others to treat you.

When people don't see each other very often, their relationships tend to become more surface-level, so their conversations usually stay on neutral topics, such as work, school, community happenings, or sports. Of course, some family members will be exceptions to this general rule. If they haven't seen you for a while, they may take the visit as an opportunity to dump all their pent-up feelings on you or criticize you and your lifestyle. However, in most cases, people do not feel as comfortable making negative comments to someone they don't see much, as opposed to someone they see frequently.

In a case where you feel the need to create boundaries or distance from a family member but are uncertain about which restrictions are right, seek professional help. Don't try to make these decisions on your own. It is easy to become highly emotional about circumstances that involve family members, which makes it difficult to arrive at objective decisions. Talk to a trusted counselor, pastor, or support group leader about the situation to get their insight and advice about how to handle it. They can assist you in establishing boundaries that will help you protect yourself from the wrongdoings or abuse of another person.

YOU AND YOUR SPOUSE SHOULD HANDLE YOUR OWN FAMILIES

Part of working through issues and establishing boundaries is deciding who should address the problem. When you are married, you need to deal directly with your own family and your spouse needs to deal directly with theirs because you each know your own families best. This should especially be the case if you are newly married. If you have been married for twenty years and suddenly your wife and sister develop a problem after enjoying years of friendship, then they will likely need to work out the issue between themselves. By this time, they have formed their own relationship, so spouses probably do not need to be involved. However, if you and your spouse have been married for only a short while or haven't formed deep connections with your in-laws, then each spouse should speak to their own family to address any issues that come up.

This procedure would still apply when there is a need to go to a person privately to resolve a misunderstanding or offense. In instances where someone has an issue with a mother-in-law or father-in-law, it is up to their spouse to deal directly with the parent. In-law relationships should be protected because they are more fragile and can be damaged much more easily. Suppose you and your husband have been married for about four months, and your husband feels he has begun to develop a good relationship with your father and two brothers. Then, he discovers through social media postings that your father took your brothers to a Major League Baseball game in your city, and he wasn't invited to join them. He is feeling a bit left out, especially since he is now officially a member of the family and you all live near one another.

After hearing about the situation, if you tell your husband, "That's between you and my father; you will have to deal with it," that is not a good solution, nor will it promote positive family relationships or a healthy marriage. By handling this issue with your father directly, you can help to facilitate good relationships between your spouse and your side of the family. The relationship you have with your father will make it easier for you to approach him about the issue. This is not to say you should leave your spouse out of the mix. You should always have open communications with him. There should not be any secrets. This is about approaching your family to solve problems so there isn't any friction between your spouse and your family.

It is up to you to talk to your father and gently let him know how disappointed your husband felt to be left out of the trip to the ballpark because he wants to be included as part of the family. Suggest to your father that he invite your spouse when he goes to baseball games with your brothers in the future. Hopefully, your father will see things from your husband's perspective and want to make things right. You can't force your father to include your husband on outings. However, your duty is to foster positive relationships between your spouse and your family if at all possible. This will also help your husband to feel honored and loved as your spouse.

IN-LAW RELATIONSHIPS SHOULD BE PROTECTED BECAUSE THEY ARE MORE FRAGILE AND CAN BE DAMAGED MUCH MORE EASILY.

YOUR SPOUSE ALWAYS COMES FIRST

Always keep in mind that your spouse comes before the rest of your family. Once you are married, your relationship as husband and wife becomes a higher priority than your relationships with other family members, including your parents. You put the marriage first to protect it. God tells us that once a man and woman are married, they leave the home of their parents and unite with one another:

> *That is why a man leaves his father and mother and is united to his wife, and they become one flesh.*   (Genesis 2:24)

Don't allow other family members to interfere in your marriage. If you have a parent or another relative who likes to criticize your spouse or undermine your relationship with them, then you need to talk to that person. The criticizing will not only make your spouse feel bad, but it might actually cause you to look down on your marriage partner because you likely respect or care about the opinions of your family members.

It is not helpful for parents to criticize their adult children's spouses. They should support their marriages by lifting up both their children and the people they have married. If you find that your family can't be supportive, then you need to create boundaries so that you put a hedge of protection around your relationship with your spouse. Remember, once you are married, you are to give first priority to your husband or wife. Your other family members now take second place. This is the way it must be in order for your marriage to be preserved and your spouse to know and feel they are the most important person in your life.

WE CHANGE OUR BEHAVIOR WHEN THE PAIN OF STAYING THE SAME BECOMES GREATER THAN THE PAIN OF CHANGING. CONSEQUENCES GIVE US THE PAIN THAT MOTIVATES US TO CHANGE.
—DR. HENRY CLOUD AND DR. JOHN TOWNSEND,
MARRIAGE AND PARENTING AUTHORS

AFTERWORD: FAMILY MATTERS

Your family relationships matter. You likely became the person you are, in large part, due to your family's influence on you. We all have a need to belong to a family and feel valued by our family members, even when we are adults. Our family interactions *should* make us feel wanted and loved. But as we know, every family has its problems, conflicts, and dysfunctions. How we handle these issues affects our long-term relationships with our family members. The sooner we learn to respond to problems according to the guidelines of God's Word and other sound principles for establishing and maintaining good family relationships, the better off our relationships will be.

It is clear that we cannot control how other people act and react. However, we are responsible for our own actions and reactions. I encourage you to use the solutions and recommendations offered in this book to help you better prevent the occurrence of the six hidden behaviors that destroy families and to produce a positive outcome when the behaviors surface. You can make a difference by providing the necessary wisdom, love, and practical solutions that your family needs to be strong and unified.

Remember, all it takes is one person to start the trend of correctly responding to mistakes and wrong behaviors so that family relationships won't be damaged but rather grow and thrive. Your actions can help your other family members to feel wanted, loved, and valued. Perhaps God has called you to be the one who will make a significant difference in the life of your extended family. Will you begin today?

ABOUT THE AUTHOR

Dr. Magdalena Battles is a writer and conference speaker whose specialties include parenting, child development, family relationships, domestic violence, and sexual assault. She shares her real-life experiences and professional insights on her website, LivingJoyDaily.com, and on Lifehack.org, where she was named one of their top writers. She is also the author of *Let Them Play: The Importance of Play and 100 Child Development Activities*.

Dr. Battles earned a bachelor's degree in child psychology and a master's degree in professional counseling, both from Liberty University, and a doctorate in clinical and academic psychology from Walden University. She has also completed postgraduate studies on "Technologies in Education" at Harvard University.

While she may seem all business, in her spare time, she enjoys camping with her family, visiting national parks, reading nonfiction, decorating, organizing, shopping, incubating and raising Silkie chickens, and spending time with extended family. She is also an active volunteer in her community and church. Dr. Battles and her husband, Justin, reside in Texas with their daughter, Brielle, twin boys, Alex and Charlie, a dog named Max, and a Silkie chicken named Marshmallow.

http://www.LivingJoyDaily.com

https://www.facebook.com/groups/DrMagdalenaBattles/

https://www.lifehack.org/author/dr-magdalena-battles

Welcome to Our House!

We Have a Special Gift for You

It is our privilege and pleasure to share in your love of Christian books. We are committed to bringing you authors and books that feed, challenge, and enrich your faith.

To show our appreciation, we invite you to sign up to receive a specially selected **Reader Appreciation Gift**, with our compliments. Just go to the Web address at the bottom of this page.

God bless you as you seek a deeper walk with Him!

WE HAVE A GIFT FOR YOU. VISIT:

whpub.me/nonfictionthx

WHITAKER
HOUSE